You Can't Fall Off the Floor

GIVE HOPE'.

Acts 20:24

I L: CD

You Can't Fall Off the Floor

Lessons I Learned While Getting Up

By
Kevin Pledger

KPP
KINGDOM PUBLISHING PRESS

Published in Nashville, Tennessee, by Kingdom Publishing Press

This book may be ordered through booksellers or by contacting:
Kingdom Publishing Press
www.KingdomPublishingPress.com
Or directly at the Author's website:
www.KevinPledger.com

ISBN: 978-0-9896330-6-2

Library of Congress Control Number: 2014921759

Printed in the United Stated of America

Table of Contents

Michelle Pledger

There are no words to describe how much you mean to me. Were it not for you, I would not have even been here for God to do what He has done in my life. Your love and prayers have been invaluable. There isn't one thing in my life that would mean even half as much if you weren't a part of it. I look forward to sharing all that God will do in our lives in the years to come. I love you.

Dedicated to:

- *Michelle, my wife.* *I can't imagine a Godlier example of a woman than you. I look at my mistakes and wonder with sheer bewilderment why you would love a man like me. I remember praying and asking God to show me how He crafted you specifically for me. I couldn't begin to draft the list that He's provided. It's quite extensive. Seemingly every day there's something new. Thank you for loving me and praying for me. You have literally saved my life more than once both emotionally and physically. I love you with all my heart.*

- *Mom & Dad (Ron & Linda Pledger).* *You guys have shown me love when I was unlovable. You would probably say that it's what any parent who loves their child would do. But not all pray as you have. Not all stand with their children as you have with me. Thank you for being shining examples of God's love to me and your church. I love you both.*

- *Roger & Nadine Waters (my in-laws).* *Not many guys can brag honestly about their in-laws, but I can! You guys have shown me so much grace and love instead of what I've deserved. I love you for that. And thank you for giving Michelle to the world and blessing our marriage. The person she is only bears testimony to the people you are. I love you both.*

- **Debby Berry**. *There are chapters in this book whose titles bear the very words you spoke into me in my deepest, darkest times. The book's very title is an example. The encouragement, grace, and truth that you have spoken into Michelle and I have been invaluable! We love you, Debby. Who would've thought that those phone calls bringing me on as a worship songwriter with PraiseCharts would have turned into THIS?!? Only God, girl. "God is so good. And He adores us."*

- **Jamie Brandenburg**. *Dude, you have brought so much more than friendship into my life! You're a brother! Our relationship, though still new, already soars high in value to me. God has used you to stir hope in a broken man. I want to follow in the example that you are setting and pour into others as you have me. Thank you for teaching me more about grace and the merciful relationship I could have with Daddy. He's proud of you too. Love you, man.*

A Special Thank You

The author thanks the following people for previewing, editing, and helping to make this book a better book.
Ted Smith
Amy Jackson
Judy Greene
Rhonda Tutt-Henderson
Ron Pledger
Linda Pledger

Introduction

The book you hold in your hand could easily be one of two things: an exposé of my life as a fallen Worship Pastor talking about the details of a life of low self-esteem, adultery, rejection, addiction, sabotaged relationships, and multiple threats of suicide; OR it could be a very long, glorified Christmas letter listing in detail the forgiveness of God and my wife to me, the blessings He has poured out on us, the healing we have found, and the joy we now walk in, so that we sound all perfect and sprayed with holy, as most of those letters do. I want this book to be neither. Instead, I want this book to be an introduction.

I made the decision to follow Jesus, or as many in the church world would call it, "get saved," at the age of 11. There is no doubt in my mind that my last breath on this earth will be quickly followed by my first breath in heaven. I am a Christian, a child of God.

But as you may have surmised by the way I opened above, there have been some poor choices along my journey. The best of friendships have been lost, people hurt that I care about, and a mockery made out of my faith. All of this was done at my own hand. I heard the cutting remarks, the comments of "you're just reaping what you have sown," and I found myself shunned by many who were Christians citing scripture and saying they didn't need influences like me in their lives. They told me that I was the reason people thought Christians to be hypocrites.

So I walked away from the Church for a period of time and tried to do life a different way. I thought that maybe my Christian friends had been right. Maybe I had character flaws that prevented me from ever being qualified to serve in the Church again in any capacity. So I came to terms with that.

I made new friends that didn't attend a weekly church service of any kind. I would tell my new unchurched friends about my experiences with my past Christian friends who had walked away saying that I was the reason people don't believe in Jesus or go to a church. Their question to me was, "What about the forgiveness you guys preach? Where is that?" I found that I received more grace, as I understood the definition, from this set of friends than I ever had from my church friends. They didn't think what I had done was excusable; they simply recognized their own failures and refused to throw a stone when they weren't perfect either.

I really didn't know how to answer that question. Is Christianity something that you join, but mess up or you're kicked out? Is there really anything to forgiveness or grace, or are those just words in a hymn? Are the rules regarding grace and forgiveness different for people who are leaders in the church than they are for people who just come and sit in the pew each week? Because if none of these questions were true, then either everything had been a lie, or I was getting railroaded.

Yet as I look down through the history of the Church in which I grew up, this trend runs solid throughout and seems to be recurring. Recording artists are found to have sinned and records are pulled off the shelf in the midst of contracts being cancelled. Preachers on TV admit to wrongdoing and they lose not only their livelihoods, but they lose their support network of friends because all of those relationships were a part of the church that they had given every waking moment of their lives to lead, the same church that has now turned their backs on them.

To all of you whose experiences have been described, who have seen the backs of countless people once called friends as they walk away, who have questioned God whether they matter anymore and are wondering if there is any way to be used going forward, I'm one of you. We walk the same road. And *you* are who I had in mind as I wrote this book.

In the pages ahead, we're going to be plunging our hands into the dirt at the very foot of the cross so deeply that the blood of Jesus must trickle down to reach our fingertips. As Christians, we have pictured ourselves at the foot of the cross, but clean. That's not an accurate assessment. The Church was never meant to be a squeaky-clean country club with a cross on it. It was, and is, a spiritual hospital for the wounded, the broken—the sinner. In other words, it's for you.

You will find in this book that you will also need to plunge into the depths of who you really are and maybe expose some hidden, dark, dirty corners of your heart. If too painful and private to expose to someone else, at least expose them to God and to yourself. These pages are not meant to excuse sin away. Quite the contrary! Sin is never excused. It is what cost Jesus His very life. To diminish sin from what it is and what it cost Jesus would be to diminish the very work that took place on the cross. I promise, that will not happen here.

If you take this challenge, maybe you'll learn to see yourself the way that God sees you—with grace. Maybe there will be lessons learned to help you know more about Christ and His genuine unconditional love for mankind, including you. And in these lessons you might see a picture of who God wants you to become by seeing first who He really is.

If you're not a Christian, as you read this book you will find that we who are Christians are not unlike you at all. We owe the world, you included, an apology.

The only thing that sets us apart is the forgiveness that we claim given through a grace we don't deserve.

Yet even this prized gift that we have been awarded by the Deity we serve isn't realized in our own lives very often, much less offered to those around us, especially each other. I look at the way that we must appear to those who don't believe as we do and say, "No wonder many don't choose faith in God." We just don't always live out the hope that we claim to have in a manner that is palatable to those around us.

I believe in a real God that loves me unconditionally. I also believe in a real devil that doesn't. I've had personal experience with both. No, I've not seen a literal God or a literal devil. I'm merely a man who is loved by one and hated by the other. A man who has seen both sides of the coin, up close and personal.

I believe there is a devil simply because I have seen the destructive power of the master of lies. What I have witnessed breathes life into the passages of scripture that tell me he is trying to intimidate me, roaring at me like a lion, and ready to pounce. The Bible says that the devil exists to steal, to kill, and to destroy. He has done all of the above in my life.

Just as I have seen the destructive power of the devil, I have also experienced the redemptive favor of God. I have felt God's love for me in ways unexplainable. I have seen Him move in ways that only an attentive Heavenly Father could for one that He calls His child. And I am a living testimony of His grace.

The one thing that I've seen in people from every walk of life is the need for some kind of hope. Everyone messes up. "I'm not perfect," we say nonchalantly. When asked how we are, we offer the expected response, "I'm fine. How are you?" And we swallow hard at the fact that we just lied.

The real matters of our lives are quite understated in the faces we portray to others. No matter whom you may face on any given day, if you could see their real behind-the-scenes story, you would see stories of despair, financial ruin, people dying with diseases, spouses and children left behind through death or divorce, the abused, the molested, the rejected, the oppressed, the enslaved, the addicted, the angry, the hurt, the broken,...the hopeless.

I want this book to bring you hope. There's nothing special about me. I have nothing to offer but the lessons I've learned as a result of my story. I'm just a person, like you, who has messed up. In society's worldview, it may be more or may be less than you. But here, in these pages, none of that matters. I needed hope. So find in my struggles strength to inspire you, a trailblazer before you who might be able to help you avoid the traps. Ride on my shoulders for a little while and take a rest. Breathe.

As I said at the beginning, I want this book to be an introduction. I learned again who I am and who He is through lessons God taught me as He reintroduced Himself to me in ways I had never known before. Get to know Him again. There IS hope. Here, let me introduce you…

Chapter 1
God Adores You

I remember sitting in my bedroom in a cloud of desperation. Just the day before, I'd had every intention on taking my life. It wasn't the first time I'd ever been there, but maybe the closest I'd ever been emotionally. Michelle, my wife, had called a counselor I'd seen years prior in the hope of him talking some sense into me. Unlocking the door to take the phone seemed to be a task that I was unworthy of performing. I didn't really want to die, but dying seemed the better of the two choices between it and living through the mess I'd made. So now, a day later, I walked out of the master bedroom into the adjoining bathroom, which had large mirrors on two walls. I looked at myself from every angle. There was nobody in that room that I recognized.

A Difficult Phone Call

We all have a past. Technically speaking, you started reading this book in the past. Every split second takes us further into the future and leaves a string of moments in its wake. For many of us, we have a past we're not proud of. The past consists of scenes that flash through our minds on a daily basis playing a film in high definition reminding us of our weakest moments, our times of which we are most ashamed, or seasons of searing hurt. For some of us, years separate the present from those moments. For others, it's only a matter of minutes. Some of you may find yourselves reading this in a desperate cry for hope because you're in one of those times right now! My past hadn't even made it to the back seat, much less the rear view! And it was time to start coming face to face with some of the consequences.

Debby is a wonderful, Godly woman that I first met when she was Vice-President for PraiseCharts. I knew this phone call would disappoint her. I strongly dislike disappointing others, but neither could I allow my life jumping the rails due to my poor decisions cause damage to the integrity of a company with which I was affiliated. My phone had never seemed so heavy.

When Debby answered, I knew I wouldn't be able to hide what was going on. Sin had ravaged me yet again. It was never supposed to happen the first time...or the second, but here I was again. How do you explain sin? No matter what spin you put on it, there's never an explanation that's good enough for doing something that has made you feel and look stupid to others, especially those that you claim to love. So I made the decision to jump right into it and explain the horrors that I had welcomed into my life.

The reaction I received only partly met my preconceived expectation. Sure, there was disappointment, but there was also grace. She was stern, but loving. I told her that I didn't even know where to start putting my life back together again. I was so angry at the world during that conversation. *Was* there even a chance of putting anything back together again? Or was I doomed to be some sort of spiritual Humpty Dumpty that had fallen so many times that all the king's horses and all the king's men no longer even *cared*? Was I to the point of being *beyond* fixing?

Debby said a couple of things that stuck with me. She said, "There's no doubt, this is a mess you've made. But there's nowhere to go from here except up. You can't fall off the floor." Her next words hit me right in the chest. She said to me, "Kevin, God adores you."

Please understand; I grew up the child of a music minister who would later attend seminary and transition to a pastor. I had been taught about Jesus my whole life. I knew that God loved me. I knew that Jesus had died for me out of love. But the word "adore" seemed to carry so much more weight, at least in that moment. When I think of that word, I hear symphony orchestras playing as cameras are flying over flowery fields, and two lost lovers are running toward each other to be reunited and live happily ever after. There was *nothing* in my life at that moment that would match up to anything worth describing as "adorable."

I "love" Alaskan King Crab. If done well, it is my favorite food on the planet. Running in a very close second is my "love" for a juicy, ripe, sweet navel orange (I don't like seeds). I "love" music. I "love" photography. I "love" a great movie in a theater with buttered popcorn. But I don't know that I "adore" any of those. Not because of what the dictionary may offer as the definition, but in my mind, the word "adore" carries such a deep kind of affectionate love. Like the mental image one would see after hearing the phrase, "worship the ground they walk on."

So while I knew that God indeed loved me, to think that He actually "adored" me seemed so unrealistic and even unattainable. I was *covered* in shame. Guilt ravaged me. Anger brewed inside me. My friends and support networks were crumbling as easily as asbestos in the hand, and with the same dangerous consequences. I was breathing it all in. I didn't even want to live. Death seemed a very welcome repose.

Have you ever been in pain like that? No matter how far in the past, whether years or seconds, pasts can be like fires. You can run or try to pull away from the sting when you feel it, but it's already on you, burning you. By the time you recognize the full brunt of the

20

pain, the mistake is made. You can't take it back. You're on fire now. And the fire uses your mind and body for fuel. As long as there's a part of you left, it seems it will never stop. And if you do get the flames put out, you stand back up only to realize you don't look like you did "before." Your past has marked you. Grossly.

This was how I felt in these moments surrounding this phone call. I was marked by my sin. There was no taking this back. I had friend after friend reminding me of that fact with each passing consequential conversation. So how could Debby say that God adored me? I wasn't *worthy* of adoration. As a matter of fact, after hanging up the phone, I began listing all the reasons I could think of why God *shouldn't* adore me. The list was long.

Following Debby, there were other calls that I made carrying the same sad story of my woes. I adopted the "I'd rather them hear it from me" attitude. In reality, I was also internally looking for someone who would sympathize with me. Maybe even someone who would tell me I was right, or at the very least, that I was justified in my actions. I found neither.

A former pastor in Illinois, Wayne, reached out to me and offered me some counseling with a licensed counselor for a weekend. While appreciated, I just had not come to the place in my life to hear from God. I'd just heard that God adores me, for Pete's sake, and I didn't care to hear that either. Hanging some Biblical wreath of truth on that door wasn't going to change much for me. I was too busy being angry and drowning in self-loathing to worry about such things. People, *friends*, were dropping me like flies and telling me that I deserved losing them as a consequence of what I'd done. I believed them. Why not? It made much more sense to me than someone, especially *God*, adoring me. I'd grown up believing that being good was supposed to be rewarded and that being bad was supposed to be punished. It was the law of the land. It was in this self-loathing that I smoldered in for the next couple of months. There is no teacher as anointed as pain to awaken the eternity within our hearts. And this pain was searing to the core.

Kairos

One day I got a phone call from Darren, a friend who pastors a church near Dallas, Texas. He and I had served together under Pastor Wayne in the same Illinois church to which I referred earlier. His current church is under the watch of Gateway Church in the metro Dallas area. He told me of a conference that Gateway offers called *Kairos* (an ancient Greek term referring to *the right or opportune time)*, and said that he would like to pay my way to come out and attend.

The last couple of months had been getting me nowhere fast. The anger, guilt, and shame were driving me further into a pit that would soon overwhelm me if not dealt with. As I mentioned earlier, I had locked myself in my bedroom threatening to commit suicide a month or so prior. If not for the actions of my wife, Michelle, calling that former counselor and passing me the phone while she prayed outside the door, I honestly don't believe this book would have ever been written, not by me anyway. My anger and sinful choices had really done a number on me. I was different and not in a good way.

So when Darren called to tell me about the conference, I took it as a sign that this was something I needed to do to stay alive. There were no other sources of hope I could find anywhere, and my prayer life was all but dead due to the fact I still wasn't to the point of genuine repentance. I was too angry with everyone who had turned their backs on me in the name of consequence. I was even angry with God for taking the sin away. At least I'd had some control over that when it was still raging. Somewhere in the back of my mind I had reached the conclusion that if friends were turning their backs on me that quickly, and if they were Christians, that surely God had done the same. Everyone had taken everything and left me with nothing. But if God was out there and if Debby had been right...as my Mom always would say, *"just in case..."*

I agreed to go to Texas for the conference. As a songwriter, I had come to respect the songwriting talent of the worship leaders and musicians at Gateway Church. Their worship staff included names like Kari Jobe, Thomas Miller, Walker Beach, and many other talented writers and leaders. I had used their songs many times while leading worship. If nothing else, I could just go and see this place that had birthed some of my most used worship tunes and possibly see some of these leaders and writers that I respected.

There were some videos I watched in preparation for the conference. They were great videos with great messages, but again, I wasn't ready to hear from God yet. Knowing my heart wasn't receptive was also concerning me about the trip. Darren was nice enough and cared enough to offer, and I didn't want to waste precious resources on something that would fall on deaf ears and maybe not do any good. Ultimately, the decision was made, so I flew to Dallas.

Rolling into the church parking lot the first day, I was strangely excited to be there. It was the first time I'd felt this way in a while about anything to do with church. The building was a sand color with large windows. The walls were wet in splotches from the rainy night before giving it almost a camouflage look. It was an extremely nice facility. The lobby had tables with snacks and coffee and water. I helped myself and made my way into the main auditorium. What welcomed me was a large rectangular room, wider than deep. The stage sat in the center with balcony stairways sweeping down and in on both sides. The largest screen I'd ever seen in a church filled the back wall of the stage with smaller "lyric screens" on the sides. I don't know how many the room sat, but thousands.

During the course of the conference, we were asked not to sit directly beside another person, but rather scatter ourselves throughout the room. Even if there were married couples there (Michelle was still in Georgia), they were to sit on opposing sides of the room so that nobody would feel eyes were looking at them in the intimate soul-searching days to come.

While there, we had several forty-five minute sessions. Each one covered different areas of our emotions that may need exploring and possibly some sort of healing. We didn't choose classes or anything of the sort. Everyone took every session together. The thought was that there might be things we were dealing with that had gone unrecognized until that moment, but they still needed to be dealt with nonetheless. I certainly realized issues I had not known existed within me until those days at Gateway. If nothing else, God had gotten my curiosity, if not even my attention. Turns out, that's all He wanted from me at the time. After all, I really had nothing else to give Him.

There were some very eye-opening moments I experienced while there, but two that I want to share with you. These two have become mile markers in my life. They are now part of what defines me and also what defines my relationship with Christ. As you will come to know in the pages that follow, it is these moments when we come in contact with a holy God that produce such mile markers. Though I didn't know to what extent at the time, I would never be the same.

The first came on the very first night. We were being led in songs of worship. The most I could do was stand and watch. Just a couple of months prior, I'd tried singing out to God. But my voice went nowhere. It had been like being in a nightmare where you're running in fear for your life. Have you ever had one of those? You want to scream or cry for help to anyone who will listen, but your fear seems to have completely left you mute. That's the best way I know to describe it.

Near the end of the worship in music time, the worship leader asked us to do some self-examination and to allow our bodies to take on the worship posture of our hearts. Worship seemed far from my ability to muster. My only thought was wondering how you get into a posture that portrays "broken." Most things that are broken are lying in pieces on the floor. So, being on the very front row of this large church, I got down on the floor and lay flat out on my stomach.

For the first time in months, I felt safe. I felt grounded. As I lay there trying to figure out what to say to God, Debby's words came back to my mind, "You can't fall off the floor." In that moment, the floor felt good. It felt stable. There was security in knowing I was as low as I could go. I was broken down to the very foundation of my being and found it extremely comforting. Besides, everything I had known before seemed just as broken as what was left of my life. Every recent day had been a blur of wrecked emotion, depression, and thoughts of suicide. It was the very definition of hopelessness.

As I lay there on the floor, the worship band started playing a song I supposedly knew very well. But once again, I could move my lips, yet the words just wouldn't come out. So I did all that was left to do. I was still. And quiet. I'd always taught that worship is born from the heart. I found myself proving those teachings to be true. There was nothing in my heart in any kind of tune with God. Worship felt absolutely impossible.

I remembered when I was a little child and having a hard time going to sleep, my mom (or dad) would come into my room and sit on the edge of the bed. I always slept on my stomach, so she would gently rub or scratch my back until I fell asleep. Lying there on the floor in the altar area of this church, I felt a hand, though not a human hand, gently rest on my back. It was the hand of God. Stay with me here because this kind of thing was foreign to me. I'd never experienced this before and would kind of look with skepticism at others who made such claims. Yet much like my mother had done, God started gently rubbing my back and putting me at rest.

I started crying as my mind raced through my mistakes, my sin. Then, as though rounding the corner on a track, my mind rounded the corner to my future worries. What seemed to be beyond the checkered flag was dismal at best. Suddenly very desperate, I started asking God questions as fast as my mind could think them. *How will I make my house payment? Where will I get money to eat? Will I still have a wife when I get home? Do I have any friends left? What's going to happen to me?* And through the worship music of the band and the engine noise of a racing mind, I heard a gentle, "Shhhhh."

God began to speak to me. He said, "You don't need to worry about any of those things right now. All I want you to do is to let me love on you for a while." I didn't think I'd heard right. I started listing again everything I could think of why that would be impossible. The list led right back to all the questions I had asked before. There was no worthiness in me I could find that would give God reason to even glance in my direction a second time. I had lost all control of everything and needed answers. Again, He gently said, "Just let me love you."

I would soon come to learn, as you will if you haven't already, that being in relationship with God is a predicator to deliverance *of* the solution and also deliverance *from* the problem. When we disappoint God, He doesn't get worried. He's God. We were created for fellowship with Him to begin with. So His main goal is a reestablishment of the relationship because He knows He *is* the solution. He is the answer. He is the healer. He told me that nothing else mattered because my every question would require an empty answer unless the foundation of my relationship with God was reestablished. I needed to be adored by Him.

Over the next couple of days of the conference, we were asked to write down areas God brought to our minds for which we needed freedom, healing and forgiveness. As I sat through the sessions, I was a student, not a former worship pastor. I brought nothing of the theology I had believed for so long into these meetings. As I sat and learned, I began to learn things about God and about myself to which I'd never given a moment's thought. My list of things from which I needed healing, freedom, and forgiveness had grown way beyond my initial expectations or even one side of a page.

As I walked through the doors into the last session, my page was chock-full. We were handed red #10 envelopes by greeters at the doors. I noticed three or four crosses standing across the front of the stage area. We were instructed to put our pages containing our lists—folded, ripped, however—into the envelopes and seal them with no names or markings on the outside.

Then we were to bring them to the front, lay them under the cross, leaving our burdens and sins at the feet of Jesus, and make our way up the center aisle to the back of the church where the staff would be waiting to pray over us and anoint us with oil. I made my way to the front and was finally able to lay my red envelope at the foot of the cross on the far left nearest where I was seated.

Walking away from the cross toward the center aisle, my mind started reeling again. I started talking to God. Actually, it may have been more like I was a lawyer making a closing argument to the jury before deliberations. I said in my mind, "This wasn't real, was it? I'm going to get home and will be hit with the same problems I had before I left. Then where are *YOU* going to be? This is just like some kind of youth camp experience where I get caught up in the emotion while away from home, then get home to 'real life' and everything goes right back to normal."

God said, "If that's what you think, turn around and pick up your envelope."

I turned and walked back a few steps to face a cross with a sea of red envelopes underneath it. Turning around again headed toward the prayer warriors, I bowed my head and said, "God, I can't tell which one is mine."

He replied, "Neither can I. Keep walking."

Empty

I had nothing left. There's a saying that says, "You can't give what you don't have." I had given out. I had no worship, no love, no money, no advice, nothing. And seemingly all my tangible friendships had walked out of my life as well. There were a few still around, but the ones you call daily or hang out with weekly; those were gone as if they had only been a mirage in the desert to begin with.

Michelle, my wife, was still there when I got home to Georgia. For some reason, she had stayed. If you asked her, and I have, she would tell you that she stayed because that's what God told her to do. She said, "I determined that I was going to listen to God and not my friends or family. God had promised He was going to bring you back around and had shown me what that relationship would look like. So I decided to trust Him and love Jesus more than you." And the strange part was, she lost her friends too. Most were angry with her for *not* leaving. Codependency labels flew freely. But in the aftermath, it was just God and us. At the time I would have wanted things any way but that one. The further I could have separated myself from facing my sin or Michelle day after day, the better off I thought I would be.

I had made my poor choices because I wasn't happy. I'd always heard from others, and had said so myself, "People deserve to be happy." Even the Declaration of Independence says we have the God-given right to "life, liberty, and the pursuit of happiness."

But see, there's the rub. I had always thought of happiness as a destination. I think most folks do. We tell each other, *"Do what makes you happy."* We say it with a determined assumption that when we do what makes us happy, we will find that place "we were meant to be" and all will be sunshine and daisies.

"You deserve to be happy." Right?

"If you want to be happy, follow your heart."

But the Bible says in Jeremiah 17:9 (NLT), "The human heart is the most deceitful of all things, and desperately wicked. Who really knows how bad it is?" The heart cannot be trusted. I had given it my trust, and it failed me. I had been so sure that I was right, but now I was beginning to see myself for the fool I'd been.

The truth is that happiness is fleeting at best. It's here today and gone tomorrow. The pursuit, as our nation's Declaration puts it, starts all over again every time we think we have it safely in our grasp. We find happiness to be too slippery to hold. That's why we are always in pursuit of it. It's not sustainable for a lifetime. We have moments of happiness, sure. If we're fortunate, we may even tip the scales and have a majority of a life lived in happiness. In reality, what we *should* pursue is contentment. You can't find contentment in the temporary that is happiness, but you can find happiness in the permanence that can be contentment. We will talk more about this later in the book.

My pursuit of contentment led me to only one thing. Love. I am loved by God. I am *adored* by God. So are you. Look what scripture says in Romans 5:8 (NLT), "But God showed his great love for us by sending Christ to die for us while we were still sinners." Let that last line sink in. *"While we were still sinners."* God didn't need me to change for His love toward me to become active. Yes, I goofed. I sinned. But God's love was bigger than my sin.

Almost everyone else in my life was waiting to see something from me to prove my repentant heart. God didn't want to see anything *from* me at all. Actually, He was more interested in *showing me* something. He knew the wages of my sin was still death. I was dying inside. The choice I had made at 11 years old to follow Him and miss an eternal death in hell wouldn't negate the death I was dying inside at present. No matter whether one has made the decision to follow Christ, the consequences of our sin will still take their toll in this life. I hadn't lost my salvation; I'd lost my identity. I was still a child of God; I just didn't recognize myself as such due to a lack of worthiness.

I found out there is such a thing as a hidden death. Please know that this is not a scriptural term; it is just my attempt to describe what I experienced. It is something that, unless you have ever been broken to your core by your own sin, you would never know or understand. Those around me were so intent on seeing me understand the external consequences of my mistakes, but the reality was that my realization of the internal consequences of my sin didn't need their help. What they felt they needed to see was actually beyond human ability to even visualize. There was an internal death. It spawned pain like I can't begin to describe.

As Christians, isn't it funny how we always think we need to help God out in enforcing sin's consequences? We always think God forgot a step and we can help Him out a little in handling people. God said there is but one step needed from us: love. True love wrapped in grace. *We* added "12 Step Programs." We proceed with the attitude that sinners had better be able to complete our 12 steps before we can even think about getting to God's one step. We act like it becomes our duty and responsibility to validate the sincerity of repentance. Who's playing the part of God in that scenario? Him or us? If there is repentance needed, we have dubbed ourselves self-appointed judges of whether it is genuine and stripped God of His holy justice. And if there is sin, we take it on ourselves to enforce consequences that we feel fit the crime. Can we not see that in taking this responsibility, we also assume the responsibility of the cross from Christ? Yet that can't be done. We're not sinless. It's an exercise in futility that breeds further destruction by creating environments where we kick our own wounded.

Though often well intentioned, we have become just like those men who caught the woman in adultery in the Bible in John 8:1-11 (NLT). They took her before Jesus. "The law of Moses says to stone her, but what do you say?" they asked Christ. Yet as many times as we've heard it, preached it, read it, we've never liked nor lived out Jesus' answer, have we? "Let the one who has never sinned throw the first stone."

I picture those people having stones in hand as they brought her before Jesus that day. They were trying to trap Jesus, yes, but they were also ready to see justice in action. They were thirsty for a good gossip story that could be offered in the guise of a prayer request for a couple of newly broken families. If you've been in church-world for any length of time, you've probably heard that done, haven't you? But the Bible tells us that Jesus knelt down after the accusers' question to Him. Before He answered, scripture describes Jesus as writing in the sand with His finger. No, we don't know what He wrote, but if I had to guess, my opinion would be that He started listing the sins of those who stood around Him with stones in hand. Whatever words were left in the dusty grains, we know that one by one, each accuser dropped his stone and walked away without another word uttered.

Notice that scripture never says *anything* about the repentance of the adulterous woman. It never insinuated that she asked Jesus for mercy or forgiveness. Only after being spoken to by Jesus, does the Bible refer to her as even speaking. After Jesus finishes writing in the dust, He stands and asks her where her accusers are. "Did even one of them condemn you?" Then follow her only words. "No, Lord." Jesus responded, "Neither do I. Go and sin no more."

There is no doubt in my mind that repentance indeed followed as she walked away. She faced *death*! But she found forgiveness, mercy, and grace. I'm sure she too felt what I have described as a hidden death. Yet in this account of an interaction with Jesus, the "villain" of the story isn't the one caught in sin, it is the collective of the *accusers*. A mess became a masterpiece in one love-filled brush stroke wrapped in grace. She experienced the adoration of her Lord. I wonder what her accusers were thinking as they walked away. Probably the same thing many of us think when we see grace applied without our prior approval.

That day in a dusty street, sin met love face to face. So did I on a floor in Texas. My accusers are still quite busy to this day. You may be one of them. They probably won't like the fact that I wrote a book, or that you're holding a copy in your hand and allowing me to speak into your life for a few moments. But I want you to know that you don't have to be worthy of God's love. Not only that, but there's nothing you could even do *to* be worthy of His love. He adores you. You are at the center of His heart. You are the very reason He took every stripe and nail that drained His life from His body on the cross. And His love is *permanent!*

Romans 8:38-39 (NLT) gives us this hope, "And I am convinced that nothing can ever separate us from God's love. Neither death nor life, neither angels nor demons, neither our fears for today nor our worries about tomorrow—not even the powers of hell can separate us from God's love. No power in the sky above or in the earth below—indeed, nothing in all creation will ever be able to separate us from the love of God that is revealed in Christ Jesus our Lord."

There are many other verses on the love of God. I have included some of those in the back of the book for you to read. My biggest desire, however, is that you would look them up for yourself in your own Bible, whether it be a physical book or an app on your mobile device. Mark these verses. Let them be real to you.

I pray you never suffer the kind of loss I've suffered, *especially* due to your own poor sinful choices. If for some reason you do or have, and you have seen careers, friends, family, support systems, finances, homes, cars, plans for the future, maybe even your church slip out from underneath you, there is hope. You can't fall off the floor. My goodness, the fact that there *is* a floor is great news. You've landed! When everything else is lost, if I (or you) would concentrate on this one thing, that we are loved, indeed we are *adored* by God, we will have found the foundation on which every other area of our lives is to be built. And there's nowhere to go from here, but up.

Lessons learned while getting up:

1. God Adores You.

What you have read is the first of a few lessons that God taught me as I was "getting up off the floor." However, as you read this book, my prayer is that God will open up new lessons to you that are personal in nature and that you might share these with others as your life becomes even more of a living testimony of hope. Use the lines I will leave for you at the end of each chapter to record those lessons along with today's date. In your future, it may help you to look back and see the actual dates that God taught you certain things.

Today's Date: _____

_____

_____

_____

_____

_____

_____

_____

_____

_____

_____

_____

_____

_____

_____

_____

_____

_____

Chapter 2
Grace: Can't Qualify, Can't Disqualify

Grace Defined

Growing up in church, I sang songs about grace. If you grew up going to church, I'm sure you did, too. *Grace Greater than Our Sin* and *Amazing Grace* were two of my favorite hymns to sing. They still are. As I would sing these songs, I knew God had given me grace in spite of my being a sinner. I speak the English language, so I knew how these songs described grace. I knew that, according to scripture, "For it is by grace you have been saved, through faith—and this is not from yourselves, it is the gift of God..." (Ephesians 2:8 NIV) What I did *not* know or understand is the definition of—the depth or the reality of—grace.

Grace is defined as: *unmerited favor.* Let's break that definition down even further.

Unmerited - *not deserved*

Favor - *an attitude of approval or liking; an act of kindness beyond what is due or usual*

So grace is undeserved approval, coupled with kindness, beyond what is due or usual. For me, I had taken in and accepted the *undeserved* part from my years growing up in church. I knew what I deserved was death, even an eternal death. I could comprehend that there was nothing I had done or *could* do that would qualify Jesus dying for *my* sin, but such was as far as my personal definition of grace had taken me. Grace was wrapped up in my inheritance as a child of God, not in anything I could receive now.

So it was the fullness of the *favor* part that I had really never grasped. The fact that I could go to heaven was certainly more favor than I deserved, so the promise of heaven pretty much wrapped up my notion of the sum total of grace. Honestly, I believe that's where most Christians put the period on their definitions as well. When we think of grace, we think more of what *will be* rather than what *already is*. We need to see the grace— the undeserved favor—of God for more of what it is in the here and now. It's not only a future tense assurance, but it's also a present tense provision.

So many things get in the way of that recognition. For me, jealousy has been a big one. I see others experiencing favor and I start replaying every scene from their sin highlight reel. It's much easier to swallow

41

the fact that someone who has hurt or disappointed us in some way has attained favor, as in eternal life in heaven, once they are dead and gone. It's a much bigger pill to swallow seeing God's favor rest on their lives while they are living it out in front of us every day. If it's happening in heaven, it's not being rubbed into our faces. We don't have to see them smile about how great their lives are when ours seem so dreary. This is especially true if we are in the middle of hurt. If God is just, and He is, then where is the justice in that kind of scenario? It doesn't seem fair, does it?

What I have learned is that God never promised fairness. There is nothing fair about grace. A person walking out of my life wasn't fair, but it *was* necessary. It wasn't fair for Jesus to die, but He did. It's not fair for anyone who has ever lived, save Christ alone, to spend eternity in heaven, but we will if we so choose by His grace. God's justice is filtered first through His grace. Ours is not. We know repentance is necessary for salvation. So it's only right for repentance to be necessary for grace, right? It would only be fair. Wrong. Grace comes *first*.

Too many of us have viewed the word *undeserved* as the lone definition of grace, but *undeserved* is in the definition more as an adjective describing *favor*. That one needs to sit with you for a moment. *Favor* is the subject of the definition. *Undeserved* merely shows us what God requires in return for His favor…nothing. Let that thought wash over you. Breathe it in. No matter what you've done in your life, this moment right now is one to savor.

Repentance is still necessary, but not before grace. The spiritual disciplines of the Church are still to be sought, but not before grace makes a way. Grace is the very thing Jesus displayed on the cross long before humanity ever knew your name. It embodies love, mercy, and forgiveness to such levels that only those who have ever found they *needed* grace can understand. When you're on the floor, you *need* grace.

By in large, the majority of well-meaning Christians that I have ever known wanted to see my repentance first. They were waiting to see if I went to the altar and cried a certain number of tears, almost as a priest who would instruct a parishioner on a number of Hail Mary's to say for penance. And even if the expectations were met, because there was still a lack of trust on their part, grace might still be withheld until my character was once again proven. There's a difference between the grace of God and the grace of most Christians. There shouldn't be. That's not a merit badge to be worn with pride.

I found that when God isolates us, as He did me, He does so for us to be able to focus solely on Him. In this case, I believe He wanted me to see His grace the way He meant for it to be seen. He knows it's not the kind of grace that so often comes from our brothers and sisters in Christ. The grace you and I need isn't carried on the wings of conditions. We just need Him. No preconceived notions. No 12 step programs. Just favor. His smile. His hand on our backs as we lay on the floor pouring out our hearts to Him in anguish and shame. His still small voice saying, "Just let me love you."

When all the distractions are removed, He is our only focus. It's like a parent needing the attention of an ADHD child and holding his or her cheeks in both hands so the child is looking right into their eyes. Now He has our attention. With our attention given, He can speak love, mercy, healing, forgiveness, encouragement, and... grace, right into our very hearts and minds.

When you find yourself so humbled by the favor of God, knowing you don't even deserve to speak His name, you come to realize that grace never makes excuses for sin. That ill-thought concept is taught throughout many of our churches today. I had a pastor actually say from the pulpit, "You show me a man who always talks about grace, and I'll show you a man looking for an excuse to sin." I strongly disagree!

Grace is no excuse. Quite the contrary. It is the primary guide leading to repentance. Reference our account from Chapter 1. Scripture never says that the adulterous woman repented before Jesus forgave her.

Grace was offered *first*. I'm very sure that repentance followed when she was on her way back home. But it was only *after* coming face to face with grace.

We have failed to take into account the fact that the sinner is a victim just as much as anyone who was hurt by the sin. Sure, the choice was theirs. I place no blame on anyone but myself for my choices. Still, the Bible describes the devil as the "father of lies" and a "master of deceit." He knows scripture better than any of us. He was heaven's worship leader at one point. On top of that, he had the audacity to try and trip up *Jesus* using scripture.

If he thinks he can fool the very Son of God, don't you think he's pretty confident in his ability to fool even the wisest among us? Haven't we already seen evidence of that in some of our most loved pastors across our nation? Oh, the first thing we cry out is that these people were some type of fraud for preaching one thing and doing another. Those thoughts in us are born purely out of blind ignorance and further deceit of the devil. Our adversary plants those thoughts within us to diminish the word of God being spoken into our lives by those who have fallen as well as others. The devil knows that if he can weaken our trust in one church leader, questions will follow about every other leader to whom we are subject in the future.

People normally don't just set out to hurt people. The majority of these church leaders would never want any hurt to come over someone they serve in their individual churches. Pain is a weapon of the enemy. The Bible even tells us that he exists to steal, kill, and to destroy (John 10:10). Pastors, Christians, people don't have problems with addictions or moral issues because they set out to hurt someone. They hurt others because they have been deceived themselves by the adversary into thinking that involvement in a sin will ease some kind of pain in their own lives. I've been that guy! I was a worship pastor, yet just like everyone else in the congregation, the enemy had lied to me and I had believed him. Anyone else who sins is in the same boat. You are, too. It doesn't end with pastors. If we're getting real, we can throw in mass murderers, rapists, child molesters, liars, thieves...you name the sin. The enemy lied to every one of those people and they believed it.

Please know that I'm not saying there is any validity to the old "the devil made me do it" excuse. There's not. The Bible is very plain. 1 Corinthians 10:13 tells us that God will not allow us to be tempted to sin beyond what we can bear. It also goes on to say that He will *always* provide a way out. So if we give in to the temptation, we are still responsible for the Biblical and/or lawful consequences that follow.

But when the people of God shun one of their own, *anyone* for that matter, they do two things that are extremely dangerous. First, the shunned person feels hopeless having lost their support network and finding themselves under the condemnation of the ones he or she thought to be friends. In such hopelessness, they will seek acceptance from somewhere. God created us to be relational. It is our nature to seek relationship. If they don't find it within the church, if there is not grace or forgiveness within those walls, they will seek other places. I did.

Second, the person will be isolated and alone. Loneliness can lead to all sorts of issues. Addictions can be formed. Suicide rates are much higher among lonely people, especially around holidays or other important dates in one's personal life. Being lonely messes with one's mental stability. It becomes a personal hell that torments the one in its grasp. Prisons even use loneliness as a form of punishment for inmates who need to be disciplined. They are sent to solitary.

There is strength in numbers. One of the reasons Christ instituted the Church is because He knew we would be much stronger as a unit in relationship with one another than we would ever be alone. Scripture says that the devil is walking about like a roaring lion seeking someone to devour (1 Peter 5:8). Lions normally don't attack their prey as long as the numbers of the herd protects the prey. They wait until their prey gets accidentally separated or injured and is found isolated.

When separation happens, weakness results. Then the carnage begins.

Satan knows that he cannot defeat the Church. The Bible is clear that the very gates of hell cannot prevail against her. But it speaks of the *collective* Church—the herd, if you will. Let one of the Church become isolated for whatever reason, and suddenly they are ripe for the pickings.

Please consider this question. Could it be that we are so hard on our own and are so quick to shun them, not offering grace first, because *the Church* is actually the ones being deceived at that point? Could it be that in the name of protecting the reputation and name of Jesus, we are destroying the very reputation we are so determined to protect?

I get why it happens. We use the scriptures about not entertaining sin and not mixing ourselves with sinners or, we too, will be tempted and sucked down. It's the Biblical equivalent to "one rotten apple spoils the bunch." That is so very much within the character of our enemy to fool us into thinking that we are acting Godly when in truth, we are the furthest things from it. In reality, we are setting our brothers and sisters up to be devoured. The devil can't take us down as a collective group, so he creates scenarios and leads Christians through temptations that eventually lead to one of us being isolated. We've believed the lie. We wandered or got injured. And now, he can take the one out without having to mess with the whole.

The whole thing could have been avoided if only the Church had offered grace first and had circled the wagons around our wounded or confused brother or sister. If we had offered love, grace, forgiveness, accountability, and protection, there would never have been the carnage that resulted. In the name of protecting ourselves, we send our own Christian family members to their slaughter. Sure, they messed up and got caught in sin. But if you take a real look in light of holiness at your own life, you will realize the only difference between them and you is that their sin has come to light. Yours is still in the dark.

Grace brings about hope when it meets the heart of the sinner. I needed that hope. I felt so hopeless that I started going down a path I was never meant to travel all because I thought it was my only choice. I was being told that I didn't deserve grace—that I needed to prove myself before being forgiven. And it was my Christian friends who were telling me these things. I have to believe they actually thought they understood what scripture said to do and acted accordingly. To think otherwise would simply make them evil and cruel, and I can't go there. But a sinner with no hope is permanently lost. Jesus painted a picture of His response, and what ours should be as well.

99 and 1

"Look at it this way. If someone has a hundred sheep and one of them wanders off, doesn't he leave the ninety-nine and go after the one? And if he finds it, doesn't he make far more over it than over the ninety-nine who stay put? Your Father in heaven feels the same way. He doesn't want to lose even one of these simple believers." (Matthew 18:12-14, The Message)

I think it's quite interesting that Jesus likens us to sheep. When it comes to animal intelligence, sheep can't claim to have the sharpest knife in the drawer. When compared to other animals, they are quite dumb in many regards. They can't think for themselves much. Attention spans are low. Even when grazing, they will eat themselves into oblivion ignoring the bloating pain they feel in their bellies. Digestion can't happen until they lie down, yet they won't lie down on their own. They must be made to lie down. (I won't go into it here, but read Psalm 23 again knowing that little tidbit of information and see if there isn't some new insight to its meaning in your life.)

I had always thought that the one for which the shepherd left the ninety-nine was in the category that the church world calls "lost" (meaning someone who does not trust in Jesus as their Savior or that they have never chosen to be a Christ-follower). But that's not what Jesus was saying here at all.

The "one" was first a part of the hundred. Look at the very end of the passage. The lost sheep was a "simple believer." He was a full-fledged part of the flock already. Initiation completed. Name on the dotted line. Wool imparted. Black socks doled out. This was a sheep. But for some reason, it wandered off. It was isolated. Separated. Alone.

The majority of the Church will tell you that we don't believe in a God that carries a lightning bolt waiting to strike down the heathen sinner who slides his toe across the spiritual out-of-bounds line. But the story quickly changes, if it's one of our own who messes up. Suddenly it's almost like the whole lot is pointing not only to the mess, but the mess-er.

We can't believe that one of our own would act in such an unbecoming manner of the name of Christ. "Why, scripture tells us we're to have no part of someone who does stuff like that," we'll cry. Matthew chapter 18, from which the above passage is taken, is often referred to as being about "church discipline." Discipline isn't the focus at all. The chapter was never meant to be a scriptural switch with which to spank a child who has stepped out of line. It's a chapter on how to be *redemptive* with someone. It's meant to be a rescue attempt.

When shepherds watched over sheep, they carried a staff. It was pointy on one end and had a crooked hook on the other. The staff had three purposes.

First, it was a way for the sheep to see the shepherd. It stuck high in the air and was taller than the shepherd, so it was easier for them to be able to follow him when they were walking in tight formations with other sheep all around.

Second, it was a weapon. Wolves would be out trying to kill the sheep for a tasty meal. The shepherd, who genuinely loved his sheep, would use the pointy end of the staff as a weapon against impending predators.

Third, it was a tool of rescue. Sometimes the sheep would be about to get into danger, or would be in water and couldn't swim. The hook on the other end would be used to reach out and hook the endangered sheep and pull him to safety. Jesus was addressing shepherds here. They knew *exactly* what He was saying and telling them about the character of God. Matthew 18 is Him stating the same thing in a different way. It merely shows how we should respond as a group versus His response as our Shepherd.

When we stray, God doesn't leave the ninety-nine to come and execute His wrath on us for wandering off. No! The wages of our sin, our wandering, are still death. There is real impending danger. The eternal part is handled if you're a believer, but not the earthly temporal. There are still earthly consequences to our sin. God knows the wolf (the devil) is out there, and this predator has been waiting for one to get separated from the herd in order to have easy prey. The shepherd's leaving the ninety-nine is not to punish the wandering sheep; it's a *rescue mission*.

He comes running, calling our names, and seeking us out. When He finds us, He doesn't rush over to us yelling at us. He knows that would startle us into thinking He is angry. Instead, He lovingly, gently calls us back to Him. If and when He gets our attention, He scoops us into His arms and carries us back to the ninety-nine so that the family is under His safe watch again.

Now here's the hard part, yet it's a beautiful picture at the same time. The shepherd then breaks the leg of the sheep. Why? He does it because though sheep may be extremely dumb animals, they have remarkable hearing. So he takes away their ability to run away by breaking their leg, but then he holds them and nurses them lovingly back to health. As the shepherd does this, he always carries the sheep in his arms with the sheep's ears over the left side of his chest. See, that's where his heart is. A sheep, when used to hearing the shepherd's heartbeat, won't stray outside earshot of that heartbeat when it's once again released on its own.

What the Heavenly Father decides to use to "break our leg" is completely at His discretion. The pain is never permanent and is always for our good. My friend, discipline is never easy. But neither is it issued from God out of anger. When you ask for forgiveness from God, rest assured that His love is immeasurable and comes wrapped in immeasurable grace. If your church family doesn't love on you and protect you, as they should, I will tell you from experience, the love of God is enough. You are still His child and at the very center of His heart. Don't give up. Don't become bitter at others. Just let Him love you. Let Him speak into your life. Get acquainted with His still small voice all over again. But most of all, know that you are not alone.

A Realization

My straying didn't cost me my status as a sheep. And my Shepherd cared so much that He came on a rescue mission to find me. And find me, He did. I was under the impression from my guilt and the voices of most of those around me that I had messed up beyond the reach of being used of God, at least in *this* lifetime.

Not too long ago, I read things that people were saying about my past that were quite stinging. I had found grace in the arms of God, yet I began to question again if what they were saying was really what my Heavenly Father thought of me. I prayed and asked

God His thoughts on the matter. More than anything, I needed His voice in that moment, and He didn't disappoint.

He said, "Son, you first need to know that I love you and I'm proud of you. Second, know that when you asked me for forgiveness, I gave it. Every sin was washed under the blood of Christ, and it wiped your slate clean. I separated that as far away from me as the East from the West, and I don't even remember it anymore. So when you hear a voice reminding you of your past, it's never Mine. That's always the voice of the enemy. How can I remind you of something that doesn't exist anymore and that I can't even remember?"

Whoever you are, whatever you've done or not done, grace has found you. It is what the Shepherd brings with Him in His heart on every single rescue mission. *Nothing* can separate you from the love of God, remember? You're still a sheep, a believer. Nothing can disqualify you from that status.

But neither can anything that we have done qualify us for grace. We have no righteousness on our own. All of our righteousness, our goodness, comes solely from Jesus. So how can we then lose what was never ours? In the depths of our sin, we are no more or less righteous than we are in the height of our holiness. Holiness is what we aspire to, not righteousness. It's not about being good. It's about becoming holy. Righteousness is given because of grace.

Therefore, when scripture speaks of being "blameless," if you have accepted the free gift of grace through Jesus' death on the cross, you are defined as *blameless*. "So now there is no condemnation for those who belong to Christ Jesus." (Romans 8:1 NLT) How can God hold you accountable for something that is no longer on your record? Let's bring that closer to home. How can *we* hold each other accountable for such things?

I'd like to close this chapter by sharing a quote from one of my favorite books of all time, *In the Grip of Grace*, by Max Lucado.

"A condemned criminal was sent to his death by his country. In his final moments, he asked for mercy. Had he asked for mercy from the people, it would have been denied. Had he asked it of the government, it would have been declined. Had he asked it of his victims, they would have turned a deaf ear. But it wasn't to these he turned for grace. He turned instead to the bloodied form of the One who hung on the cross next to his and pleaded, 'Jesus, remember me when you come into your kingdom.' And Jesus answered by saying, 'I tell you the truth, today you will be with me in paradise.' (Luke 23:43)."[1]

History and personal confessions have shown us that there have been serial killers, rapists, and child molesters—those whom society deems the worst of the worst—who have made the same plea. On the authority of scripture, I believe they received the same response as the dying thief in Jesus' day. Their pleas for grace would have been just as valid as our own. Their sin, when stacked against the perfection standard of holiness, no worse than our own. The only righteousness that any of us can claim is only in Christ. All things being equal, I'm sure the response from a loving Jesus was equal, too. We can refuse to accept grace. But nothing, *nothing,* disqualifies you or me from grace.

Sin ravages.

Grace restores.

Hope results.

Lessons learned while getting up:

1. God Adores You.

2. Grace: Can't Qualify. Can't Disqualify.

What lessons did God teach you as you read this chapter?

Today's Date: _____

_____

_____

_____

_____

_____

_____

_____

_____

_____

_____

_____

_____

_____

_____

_____

_____

_____

_____

_____

_____

_____

_____

Chapter 3
There's Strength In the Journey

Start with Truth

The nature of any darkness is to stay dark. Can we agree with that? If any light comes into the darkness, darkness ceases to exist. Light *always* overtakes darkness and obliterates it. Such is true with sin. Not that we always sin at nighttime, but sin fears truth just as darkness fears light. Darkness (sin) will fight you to stay away from light (truth) so that it can continue to thrive.

Truth and light are necessary. They reveal *who* we are and *where* we are. In John 8:32, scripture tells us that *the truth shall set you free.* While I fully believe that to be true, I also believe it must be maintained over the entire journey. It's not a one-time decision, but a daily one. As truth shines light into the dark corners of our hearts, we begin to see revelations that explain things. We see things like unresolved tensions, unconfessed sin, broken relationships, and issues with character.

I'm inviting you to make a journey. You are already where you need to be for embarkation. No matter where you are, this journey must start from right there.

There's no right or wrong starting point. As with any journey, the goal of making it lies in the final destination, not where you begin. Starting points determine some factors *about* the journey, but they do not define the *success of* the journey.

In the first two chapters, you have probably learned a few things about yourself. Hopefully, most of them have been positive and you have determined to walk in the grace that Jesus has freely supplied to you. So before the first step of the journey begins, in light of these newly revealed truths, proper preparations need to be made. Forgiveness may need to be sought. Restitution made. Confessions told. There must not be anything hidden. Nothing dark can hide when light is introduced. Darkness only provides the cloak in which our secrets remain secrets. As much as it may anger or hurt you to do so, you must come clean with God, yourself, and others. This helps you to understand the reality of where this journey will begin for you. Think of it as a conditioning of your character for what is to come.

Beginning with anything other than what's real will distort the rest of the journey. It's like planning a trip from Atlanta to Orlando, but starting in Nashville. You know exactly the route to take, the gas needed, and the drive time from Atlanta, but you've failed to accommodate for the added mileage from Nashville. You're going to not only come up short, the roads won't be where they're supposed to be, it will take you much longer, and there will be mountains in the way for which you didn't account.

Take an honest assessment of where you are physically, spiritually, and emotionally. You might not like what you see, but if you don't know where you are, you'll never properly get where you want to go. When you know the defined starting point and a determined destination, the route will make sense. There will be a traveling time, stops along the way, bathroom breaks, refueling, eating; but at the appointed time, you should arrive safely.

We must have clarity of understanding of our measurement of truth. That would be like picking up any old object you can think of and trying to use it for a map. Truths are defined by their effectiveness and integrity. We cannot say "well, this may not be true for you, but it is for me. You use that map of Colorado and I'll use this one. Mine looks a little more like New Jersey, but I'm sure they'll get us to the same place. A map is a map is a map, right?" Sure, there are relative truths. In relative truth, one truth must be true in order for the next to be true. But even in relative truths, there must first be a foundational truth on which the rest are based. We cannot think that there are all kinds of foundational truths from which we may choose and successfully navigate the journey. Call it a moral compass, a list of standards, or what have you. There is but one foundational truth, one standard by which we must aspire to live and travel life's journey. That truth, for me, is a person - Jesus. It's not a feeling or an instinct of the heart. Neither of the latter have the effectiveness nor the integrity to withstand the tests which truth must uphold.

Know Where You're Going

I met Jamie through a friend of a friend on Facebook. We sat down over coffee at a local Starbucks a few months after Michelle and I moved to Nashville, Tennessee. Jamie is an entrepreneur, a great leader, and a mentor with a servant's heart. I was thrilled to just have another guy with whom to have coffee for an hour or so, but Jamie has become a great friend. I needed one of those.

"So tell me about Kevin Pledger," he said after the initial niceties. I'd never met him face to face until now, so I didn't have anything to lose. I told him about me. I went into detail (as much as you could in about an hour) of all the ugliness that had been my life and the healing that had begun on an altar floor in Dallas.

One of the things I like about Jamie is the way that he refers to God. He simply calls Him "Daddy." I'd never heard anyone do that before, but it is so intimate and indicative of the relationship I believe Jamie to have with our Heavenly Father.

I'll never forget one of the first things Jamie said to me after I told him my story. He said, "Bro, I feel like Daddy wants me to tell you something. I feel like He really wants me to tell you that He's proud of you." My eyes started to water. They do now even remembering the conversation. Daddy? *GOD?* Proud of *me?*

It just didn't seem possible. My mind was whirling with emotion. I don't know if Jamie said anything else right after that, or if he gave me a few moments to let that thought sink in. If he said something, I couldn't even begin to tell you what it might have been. The thought was too overwhelming.

If most of the people who had walked out of my life had been sitting there at that table, some would have gotten angry with Jamie after such a proclamation. Others would have called him an "enabler" for telling me such a thing when I needed discipline, structure, and accountability in my life. Heck, my very best friend that I'd known for over thirty years told me that I needed to be in an institution, and until I had submitted to that kind of accountability, that he could not be friends anymore. He still refuses to speak or have anything to do with me to this day.

Could *ALL* of them have been wrong and Jamie be right? Could God really be *proud* of me? YES! And He's just as proud of *YOU*. That's the very definition of grace, remember? Undeserved... *favor*.

Jamie and I started meeting about once every week or two, depending on schedules. I found that He and I have a common passion for the study of leadership. Leadership is a spiritual gift of mine. I love it and love to teach it. Something that is common in leadership circles is for leaders to make a five to ten-year plan for their organizations. The great ones may also do such plans for their personal lives. I have taught this many times.

"So how long has it been since you've done a five-year plan for yourself?" Jamie asked one day. I was embarrassed to say that it had been about 15 years. I'd spent so much time teaching others, I'd forgotten that I must first be a great student before I can be a great leader.

"What are you doing this afternoon?" he added.

"Nothing today," I replied. "I have the afternoon off from work."

"Great! I want your five-year plan in my inbox by 8:00 tonight."

"Well, alright then. I guess my afternoon just filled up."

I'm going to be honest with you. I didn't even know where to start. I remember going home, picking up my computer, sitting in my chair and just staring at the screen with a blank, frightened look. I *knew* God had brought me to Nashville, but I really hadn't known why.

I wanted to ask, but felt ridiculous in doing so. What right did I have to make a plan for my life anyway? Who was I to tell God what to do with me?

Then it hit me. *Man* said, "If you ever want to make God laugh, tell Him your plans." *God* said, "Where there is no vision, the people perish..." (Proverbs 29:18a KJV). The "vision" spoken about in this scripture passage, in other translations, can also read "divine guidance," "word from God," or "revelation." A just God would never instruct His people in a way that is impossible for them to fulfill. Such an act wouldn't be justice. To me, this verse is saying that there is indeed a way that I can receive a vision, some divine guidance, a word from God, a revelation about my life.

So I went about the complicated task of getting something from a holy God. In other words, I simply asked. (Sometimes we make a relationship with God so complicated, when He has told us to simply ask.) As I sat there in my chair and prayed, I searched my own heart. The questions I asked myself that day were a little different; but as I've helped others through this process since then, I've boiled these questions down to two that I'd like you to answer right now. These are not original to me. Many have used them before. Get a pencil (not a pen in case you make a mistake). After time in sincere prayer, write down your answers to these questions on the lines provided.

1. Your obituary is the paragraph that appears in publications after your death giving a brief overview of who you were and the things accomplished in this life. On the lines below, write out your own obituary. Before you write, think about *the most important* things for which you want to be remembered.

_____

_____

_____

_____

_____

_____

_____

_____

_____

_____

2. Your epitaph is the *one brief line* that actually appears on your tombstone and sums up your life in one sentence. Write that line below.

_____

_____

This sum total of these two answers is your destination. It is your target. If you don't have a destination mapped out, *any* direction will do. As with any journey, to reach the destination you *must* move first. You can't close your eyes and make a wish and magically arrive. A vision is simply a wish that decided to take the first step. So take a realistic look at where you are now, point the arrow at the target above, chart the course, and take a step. Turn your wish into a vision.

If it is a worthwhile plan, it will take you outside your comfort zone. It will challenge your character and test your resolve. It will stretch your preconceived limits about yourself. To make a plan that doesn't stretch you is only planning to fail. Making plans that *will* stretch you—plans that require resolve, effort, and perseverance—will end in positive results. That's the key point to the journey. The process makes us stronger. Without the process, the journey, we aren't fit for the destination upon arrival.

If at some point you find yourself asking why God hasn't blessed your vision, start by asking yourself if your vision has a focus on others. Others are at the center of His heart, and they should be at the center of yours, too. It's perfectly okay to seek to fulfill the dreams that God has placed inside you. He gives them to you, and He expects you to use them. But God never sends us on a journey alone. At the least, we have Him with us.

However, along the way, there will be others with whom we will interact. Consider them divine appointments; people placed in our path by God's design.

The first few verses of Romans 5 say this; "Therefore, since we have been justified through faith, we have peace with God through our Lord Jesus Christ, through whom we have gained access by faith into this grace in which we now stand. And we boast in the hope of the glory of God. Not only so, but we also glory in our sufferings, because we know that suffering produces perseverance; perseverance, character; and character, hope." (Romans 5:1-4 NIV)

Romans tells us that it is our perseverance through hard times that builds character and brings hope. It is said that there is no *testimony* without *test*. If you're reading this book, I'm sure you already know that to be true from personal experience. This is why the journey, the process, is so important. It's the journey, not the destination, which gives us our story of how we made it through to help encourage those who are coming behind us.

Stops and Markers

Even the least detailed person in planning has a general idea of stops they intend to make along a trip. I'm not very detailed unless I work at it. My parents live in Florida and I'm in Tennessee, while my in-laws and extended family are in Georgia. If Michelle and I drive to either of these locations, we have an idea of how far we can get before having to refuel, what towns have some pretty good places to eat along the way, and of what snacks to carry along in the car.

These days, most information you need can be gathered along the journey through your Smartphone. But as smart as they are, they are never so smart as to usurp the human experience. As we travel, we learn. We see scenery, visit new places, and take pictures to help us remember, share experiences on social media, try new restaurants, and learn where the cheapest gas prices are. We bank this knowledge and use it for the future.

Life is no different. The stops along the way, the mile markers when we celebrate successes, and even the road itself teach us more about who we are and what we are made of. We test and push our endurance. Discipline is found to be paramount to our successful arrival, and every mile passed makes us hungrier to conquer the next mile.

There will be speed bumps. There will be times when the GPS tells you to go one way because it has the traffic reports, but you swear to yourself that your way is better, only to get bottled up in traffic and lose time. Mistakes will be made. Just keep pushing through every trial. You will find that with every win, the losses seem much less important. You will also find strength. The strength from God will manifest itself in your faithfulness while your own strength grows through testing and momentum.

From time to time, you may be tempted to concentrate too much on the next step. Which job should I take? Should I date this person? Do I need to go back to school? What percentage of my money should I save? Should I move to another city? Look at your destination that you wrote out a few minutes ago. Will these decisions take you one step closer to that final destination? If not, you need to rethink your next step. The next step is temporary. Necessary, yes. But you're not going to stay there.

The Apostle Paul said it this way, "I press on to reach the end of the race and receive the heavenly prize for which God, through Christ Jesus, is calling us." (Philippians 3:14 NLT) The here and now is only a means to an end. It's the end of the race, the goal, the destination that is where our focus is to be fixed. We learn from the journey. But we focus on the goal.

Look at these verses from 1 Corinthians 2:9-12, "That is what the Scriptures mean when they say, 'No eye has seen, no ear has heard, and no mind has imagined what God has prepared for those who love him.' But it was to us that God revealed these things by His Spirit. For His Spirit searches out everything and shows us God's deep secrets. No one can know a person's thoughts except that person's own spirit, and no one can know God's thoughts except God's own Spirit. And we have received God's Spirit (not the world's spirit), so we can know the wonderful things God has freely given us."

Do you see it? God has given us His Spirit, which searches out and reveals to us God's "deep secrets." We have a window into the very mind of God. A window that He controls, mind you, but a window that reveals to us His higher ways and thoughts about us and His plan and purpose for our lives. I believe with all my heart that when I sat down to write my five-year plan, it was this window through which I saw what God has planned for me and will do in and through me if I remain faithful. Our faithfulness is the character that has developed in us as Romans 5 mapped out.

The Crown Awaits

After November of 2011, my career as a Worship Pastor was over—at least as I had known it to that point. 2012 was a "backside of the wilderness" year for Michelle and I. No jobs to speak of and only very little in the way of unemployment income equaled financial hardship like we had never known. So when our collective families gave to us financially that year for Christmas, we didn't know what to do with the money. There was no way to make up our mortgage. Paying the money we had to that end would have been much like throwing feathers into a tornado in order to stuff a pillow. There's no way that could happen. So what would be the best use for us at this crossroads in our lives? We prayed and asked God to reveal what He would have us do.

A couple of days later, Michelle said that she felt like we needed to spend the money to do something for us as a couple. Just get away from the madness and the memories that filled the town near Atlanta where we lived at the time. I was in full agreement. With very few exceptions that I can probably count on one hand, we hadn't even been out of the house to do anything for ourselves except go to the grocery store or church on the weekend in over a year.

Something Michelle had always dreamed of doing was going to CMA Fest in Nashville. It's the biggest country music fan festival in the nation and Nashville's number one crowd-drawing festival held each year in June. Sounded good to me. A friend hooked us up with someone who had years of experience and knew all the right things to do and places to stay.

As we looked at the ticket prices and the money we had on hand, we'd have enough for the tickets, but housing would be an equal amount. Added to the ticket price, we were coming up far short on cash. Needless to say, we were both disappointed. Then one night Michelle looked at me as we sat in our living room and said, "You know, it wouldn't be half as much to go if we actually *lived* in Nashville."

So we hatched a plan to maybe spend our money on a one-week trip to Nashville to try and find jobs and an apartment. This was a *huge* risk! This was every dime we had to our name going on a one-week gamble. But we hadn't been able to find work near Atlanta, not even bagging groceries. So in the end, what could it hurt? My experience has taught me that success most often follows one having first been a successful failure. Great gain only follows great risk, and we were about to risk it all. Yet we both felt that this was what God was leading us to do.

On the drive up to Tennessee, we were listening to one of our favorite pastors on a Podcast, Bishop T.D. Jakes. I honestly don't remember much about his message at the beginning. There were so many questions flooding my mind, wondering if we were doing the right thing. But Michelle and I both had an unexplainable peace about what we were doing. The whole thing was strange to me considering the risk and circumstances.

Then as a sound engineer would fade out one track on a mixer to bring up another, my questions faded and I started listening to Bishop Jakes intently. He was speaking about King David being on the run from the madness that was King Saul. Saul had been hunting David to kill him due to anger born out of jealousy, and David had been hiding out in a town called Ziklag.

One day a messenger, a young soldier, arrived in Ziklag with the crown of King Saul, Israel's king. When David inquired as to the meaning of this messenger having the king's crown, he was told that Saul and Jonathan, Saul's son and David's best friend, along with Saul's other sons had all perished in battle. Saul fell on his own sword because the enemy was close, and he feared them making a game out of killing him.

However, Saul did not die of his suicidal wounds. When this young soldier came upon him, Saul was barely alive and asked the soldier to finish the job. The soldier did as was requested. He then took the royal crown and bracelets and brought them to David in Ziklag.

The main point of Bishop Jakes' message that day was that God provided an answer to David's questions. For eighteen months David had been hiding out in Ziklag. And for eighteen months he was questioning why God had brought him there to that place. Now he had his answer. God had brought him there because

God knew that Ziklag was where the crown was going to be.

God spoke again very clearly to me. He told me that Nashville was where my crown was going to be. As I write this, I don't know yet what that looks like. Sometimes we have too much month for the money. But I'm trusting in the One who led me here. I'm believing that there is a purpose. Though, I'm sure there will be questions to come in days ahead, this answer has settled my current questions for me.

In case you're wondering what happened, we arrived in Nashville late Sunday night. I had found a job by Tuesday. Michelle had two serious leads by Thursday, one of which actually turned out to be where she would end up working. Friends supplied us with resources to stay a second week because we still had not found a place to live. God took care of that in a way that only He could on Wednesday of the second week.

We went home on Friday, packed our house over the next week, the last week of February 2013. We *gave* most of what we had away. But the God stories we could tell you about even *that* would amaze you. On March 5, 2013, almost two weeks to the day after putting the deposit down, we moved into our apartment in Nashville and have never been happier.

Now understand, Nashville is not the end of the story. That is a narrative known only to God right now.

I'm not sure what tomorrow holds. I can tell you with a large degree of certainty that there will be difficulties and many more questions. I don't have everything all figured out. My life is a work in progress and will be until my last breath. My encouragement to you is found in trusting God with the results. I have seen first-hand how God can work behind the scenes laying out His amazing plans before you step by step.

Just as I do, you, too, will experience questions on your journey. Unexplained reasonings and shortages of finances may cloud your mind. There will be fingers pointed by people who are just waiting for you to fail...again. Naysayers will line your way as cheerleaders do a marathon. Hebrews 12:1 tells us that a great cloud of witnesses—those who have gone on before us, surrounds us. Here, we are usually surrounded by little more than an impassioned mob of accusers. While not looking to actually end your life, there may be a drive to assassinate what's left of your character, your reputation, or your testimony. They will tell you to be realistic. They'll say your mistakes prevent you from reaching a vision so big. I have learned, however, that those who discourage you citing a lack of reality normally do so from their own lack of a vision. *Keep going!*

Dig into your strengthened resolve. It is not for them that you journey. It is not for them that you learn and experience. It is only for you to be able to experience the smile of the One who gave His life so that you might have yours, and have it abundantly. It is so that we *both* can one day hear Him say face to face, "I'm proud of you!" And *that*, my friend, is *hope*.

Don't let today's problems hide yesterday's provision or tomorrow's promise. Let all three strengthen you and your resolve. Persevere. "Press on to reach the end of the race," as Paul said, and enjoy the journey. A crown is waiting for you to arrive.

Lessons learned while getting up:

1.   God Adores You.

2.   Grace: Can't Qualify. Can't Disqualify.

3.   There's Strength In the Journey.

What lessons did God teach you as you read this chapter?

Today's Date: _____

_____

_____

_____

_____

_____

_____

_____

_____

_____

_____

_____

_____

_____

_____

_____

_____

_____

_____

_____

_____

_____

_____

_____

_____

Chapter 4
The Difference Between 'Content' & 'Enough'

Content

We've already talked about how happiness is fleeting and the fact that everyone does not deserve to be happy. Happiness is a desirable pursuit, but not a worthwhile destination because you cannot stay there. Contentment is much more worthwhile. It is stable and attainable for long periods of time.

For practically all of my life, I thought a contented person is one who has settled for something less than the best. I grew up hearing people say things like, "Just be content with what you have. Don't desire things that you don't have." While that may sometimes be true in financial circles, for someone who finds himself in pain or loneliness, being content in those circumstances seems much less than appealing, if it's even possible.

As I've stated earlier, I'm a student of leadership. A leader who is content with where his organization stands currently isn't much of a leader. He or she lacks vision for the future and drive to lead the organization to the next level. At least, that has been my experience. Leaders constantly need a target to which they are leading their organizations. They are constantly helping their teams to be better and stronger than the teams ever realized they were on their own.

What I've learned is that being content doesn't always mean being satisfied with where you are and only maintaining a status quo. It can also mean that while you aren't coveting what others around you have, and you're not settling for second best, you also agree that you will find the reason for being where you are in this present time and are going to focus on blooming where you have been planted. This point in your life is part of the journey. You are still in process. The journey is that part of the process that creates resistance. It is the challenge to your character and faith that will grow those muscles within you. These times of resistance should be welcomed within us. They teach us to persevere. And through perseverance, we develop character. And that character development produces hope.

Contentment, in the context of which I want to focus this chapter, is defined as being satisfied with that which God has chosen to bless you; that you aren't complaining because someone else appears to have more or better than you. In other words, *greed* should not be the cause of any *dis*contentment.

Discontentment, or dissatisfaction, is the leading motivator for change. I've done my best to research who said this to no avail, but *someone* said it best when they said, "Change seldom occurs until the pain of staying the same exceeds the pain of change." That pain comes from healthy dissatisfaction - a belief that you have learned all you can from where you are and that God is leading you to the next step. This is true within *any* context it is used. Change is not only necessary in life; it is *good* with the right motivation. But when change is motivated by greed, serious danger looms. This is especially true on a personal level. Families can be destroyed, dreams ruined, financial health wiped out, and physical health either damaged or taken. When greed has resided in the heart of the leader, entire nations have fallen.

Using myself as an example and being totally transparent, I care what others think about me to a fault. I like others to like me and I'm greatly troubled when they don't. But when it comes to someone that I respect or admire, or speaking of those who are in authority over me, this is multiplied ten-fold. Looking back on my life, I have seen that when people whom I have respected, or those to whom I have been responsible, have been disappointed in me for some reason, those have been the times when I have self-destructed. This is because I have been guilty of looking for my self-identity in what others have thought about me rather than what God says is true about me. (As you continue reading, you may want to ask yourself if you have been guilty of similar thoughts and read with your answer in mind.)

Greed would rise up within me as a medicine to make the pain of someone not liking me go away. I would see something that I wanted—that I thought would make me feel better about myself—and I would go after it with everything I had. I would seek those voices that would build me up and tell me things that would make me feel good about myself. I looked for people to blow sunshine in my ear, so to speak. Those actions have cost me.

Years ago, I learned the meaning of transference. Look it up. Google it. I learned that 80% of everything *bad* said about you is actually a lie. At the same time, so is 80% of everything said about you that is *good*. What people tell you about yourself is only based on their perception of who they believe you to be, not who you really are. So if only 20% of anything people say about us is true, then we'd better learn to be content with who God says we are.

There are things God can teach you right where you are, even if that place is due to a bad decision on your part. Scripture tells us that when we seek Him, we will find Him (Matthew 7:7). No matter how far you've drifted, you're never outside the earshot of your Heavenly Father. Remember, He's the Good Shepherd who has left all the other sheep just to come and find *you*.

The lesson I had to learn the hard way is that God desires even more for me than I desire for myself. God made me, made *us*, for extraordinary things. "'My thoughts are nothing like your thoughts,' says the Lord. 'And my ways are far beyond anything you could imagine. For just as the heavens are higher than the earth, so my ways are higher than your ways and my thoughts higher than your thoughts....'" (Isaiah 55:8-9 NLT) Jesus, Himself, said, "The thief's purpose is to steal and kill and destroy. My purpose is to give them a rich and satisfying life." (John 10:10 NLT)

Enough

Yet we must not confuse finding contentment in what we have with having enough. I'm honestly not contradicting myself here, even though you may be thinking that I am. Hopefully, as I continue, this will become a little clearer. It took some time for me to grasp that, too.

Knowing when you have *enough* seems like a noble thing, doesn't it? It sounds like the right thing to do. Most people think that Jesus didn't have much, so why should I seek more than just *enough*? More than that would be excessive, right? It would be more than what I need. Others would go lacking. These are all right thoughts *unless* God has instructed you to have more than what you deem to be *enough*.

Recently I've been thinking and praying about blessings. I fully believe that Michelle and I are going to be seeing abundant blessings from God in the next few years. I believe that with all my heart. I believe that God telling me that Nashville is where my crown would be means something important. It started with a questionable trip here to "Nashvegas" and continued with that challenge from Jamie in the previous chapter to do a 5-year plan for my life. When I initially wrote my plan, I felt I had over-asked what I should. I KNEW I had over-asked what I deserved. Where in that plan did I overstep the line of *enough*?

I began asking God if I was selfish. I'd asked this question before with an unmistakable response to the negative. But I had a hard time believing that God wanted to bless me to the extent outlined in my plan. It really is quite a remarkable plan. So I felt the unnecessary need to ask again if I'd out-punted my coverage, so to speak. It was in this questioning that Michelle and I (along with another friend) started a 6-week Bible study by Priscilla Shirer on the life of Gideon in the Old Testament. The first night of homework and personal study gripped me as I started to see the answer of God unfold before my very eyes. Don't you LOVE it when God answers the cry of your heart in unmistakable ways?

In order to show you what I mean, I must first lead you on a very brief journey of where I've been in scripture. Deuteronomy 7:1-2 (NLT) tells us, "When the Lord your God brings you into the land you are about to enter and occupy, he will clear away many nations ahead of you: the Hittites, Girgashites, Amorites, Canaanites, Perizzites, Hivites, and Jebusites. These seven nations are greater and more numerous than you. When the lord your God hands these nations over to you and you conquer them, you must completely destroy them. Make no treaties with them and show them no mercy."

In this passage, God's people are on the threshold of the Promised Land. Moses has led them out of Egypt. Most recently, Joshua has led them here. The words, "As for me and my house, we will serve the Lord" are already in Joshua's thoughts and not far from reaching the ears of God's people. God has said He will deliver these armies who are stronger in number and strength into the hands of His people. All they have to do to win the battle is *show up*. Then the land could change in name from "Promised Land" to "Delivered Land."

But what happens instead? To find out, let's skip ahead a little ways and read it as it happened. Read the verses that follow from Judges 1 (NLT). I think you'll begin to get the idea.

Judges 1:19, 21 - "The lord was with the people of Judah, and they took possession of the hill country. But they failed to drive out the people living in the plains, who had iron chariots. The tribe of Benjamin, however, failed to drive out the Jebusites, who were living in Jerusalem. So to this day the Jebusites live in Jerusalem among the people of Benjamin."

Judges 1:27-28 - "The tribe of Manasseh failed to drive out the people living in Beth-shan, Taanach, Dor, Ibleam, Megiddo, and all their surrounding settlements, because the Canaanites were determined to stay in that region. When the Israelites grew stronger, they forced the Canaanites to work as slaves, but they never did drive them completely out of the land."

Judges 1:29-32 - "The tribe of Ephraim failed to drive out the Canaanites living in Gezer, so the Canaanites continued to live there among them. The tribe of Zebulun failed to drive out the residents of Kitron and Nahalol, so the Canaanites continued to live among them. But the Canaanites were forced to work as slaves for the people of Zebulun. The tribe of Asher failed to drive out the residents of Acco, Sidon, Ahlab, Aczib, Helbah, Aphik, and Rehob. Instead, the people of Asher moved in among the Canaanites, who controlled the land, for they failed to drive them out.

Judges 1:33 - "Likewise, the tribe of Naphtali failed to drive out the residents of Beth-shemesh and Beth-anath. Instead, they moved in among the Canaanites, who controlled the land. Nevertheless, the people of Beth-shemesh and Beth-anath were forced to work as slaves for the people of Naphtali."

Are you getting the picture? Can you see the similarity in each one? Epic FAIL!

Each one of these failures that Judges chapter 1 outlines cost the people of God *dearly*. As a matter of fact, those very people that were not conquered, even though God promised He was going to deliver them into the hands of His people, are the ancestors of the people who give Israel a fit even to this very day. It is why we have the tension between Israel and Palestine and battles over the Gaza Strip.

The thorn in the flesh has never gone away. All because God promised a blessing, gave it to His people, His people saw iron chariots and higher numbered armies and decided that a little Promised Land was better than no Promised Land. So they settled for about half. They thought half was *enough*.

Had God not ordered *all*, half might make sense. But God saw what was to come. He knew the hearts of those whom Israel didn't fully wipe out. This is why in Deuteronomy; He said to "show no mercy." He knew that in time, there would be no mercy shown for His people in return. God is not a God that is bound by common sense or reason or even time. His ways and thoughts are higher than that. He sees all of eternity at a single glance. That's not logical or even imaginable to the human mind, yet it is as common to God as breathing is to us.

Our enemy, the devil, fooled the people of God into thinking that *some* was better than *all*, though God had both promised *all* and commanded *all*. What about those questions you wrestle with all the time? You know what I'm talking about. They are the things that you know God is telling you to do; leading you to do, and so you just do *enough*. Christians today are all about *enough*. What is *enough* service as a volunteer in my church? What is *enough* time with my kids? What is *enough* money spent on my spouse for a birthday gift? What is *enough* to give as a tithe or offering to my church? How much is *enough* forgiveness for that person that hurt me? How many good deeds are *enough* to outweigh the bad ones? Our church building is big *enough*. I've done *enough*. I've had *enough*. Just *ENOUGH*!

When did *enough* become enough to God when it comes to blessing His people? When He talks about blessing us, He speaks in terms of windows being opened and blessings poured out so that we won't have room to receive it. He talks about cups running over. He mentions an eternal heavenly inheritance. He uses words like "whoever," and "whatever." There is a promise to the seeking, asking, and knocking. There's not a "Full" marking on God's blessing gauge. It doesn't even have an "ENOUGH" about halfway up.

What God does, Himself, is the only time we can ever say that enough has been done. His creation was enough. His plan was enough. His Son, Jesus, was/is enough. Heaven will be enough. But then, in all of this, He gave all He had. There was nothing more to give.

My friend, whatever is in your past, whether it was only a few short moments ago or years, if you have asked God's forgiveness, His forgiveness is *enough* to cover it. Jesus' blood is enough, no matter what. The price that He paid on the cross satisfied the amount due. It was enough. But His love for you, His blessing that is waiting for you, His joy that hearing you speak His name brings—those kinds of things never hit *enough*. You are His child. Let Him speak into your heart and let Him tell you how proud of you He is. If there is a blessing that you don't feel worthy of that is before you, take it. None of us are worthy. If there are those who are saying that you don't deserve your blessing...well guess what? Neither do they. But that is the grace of God in action. Those blessings are His gift to us. And He wants us, in some cases even commands us, to claim them.

What is it that you have walked away from too soon because you saw something that scared you? You saw the iron chariots, and they looked quite daunting. You thought there was no way to complete the task because of the opposition even though you recognized that God presented it to you. Or there were *all those people* who said you couldn't do it, or that you shouldn't do it, and you gave up because of some form of "reality check" that you got duped into believing. DON'T STOP! DON'T QUIT! The Promised Land is just that . . . PROMISED. If God said it's yours, then HOLD HIM TO HIS WORD and TAKE IT.

Maybe the people shouting from the sidelines have you believing that what you've done and where you've been in life disqualify you from being used of God for something great. Let's look at that. 1 Corinthians 1:27 (NLT) says, "Instead, God chose things the world considers foolish in order to shame those who think they are wise. And he chose things that are powerless to shame those who are powerful."

Sometimes He just likes to use the most unusable person to accomplish the most difficult of tasks. The guy with the speech impediment to lead his people (Moses); the adulterer and murderer to be king of His people, called a "man after God's own heart," and of whose bloodline Jesus would be born (King David); a man who denied Jesus three times surrounding Jesus' crucifixion chosen as the founding father of the Church (Peter); a mass murderer of Christians chosen to write over half of the New Testament (Paul); and the list goes on and on.

But Kevin, how do I KNOW that the promise is from God? Here's how I check it. If it fails any ONE of these, I know that I'm to walk away and that the enemy is deceiving me.

1. Does it go against any part of scripture in any way? If no, you're good here.

2. Does it bring glory to God? If yes, you're golden on this one.

3. Does it have the good of others at heart? If yes, keep going.

4. Does it fall into any area of my weaknesses to sin & temptation? If no, good.

5. Is any part of it born from selfish motivation? If no, go on.

6. Would it put God in a position to show off? If yes, yippee!

7. When I tell Jesus about it face to face, will it make Him smile? If yes, it's a keeper!

I leave you with this. Be content with what God gives you and bloom where you are planted. But if He indeed gives you a blessing or promotion, *take* it. Part of obedience is in realizing there are no parts to obedience. It's all or nothing. So is the reward. The fullness of our blessing depends on the completeness of our obedience.

Obey in full and be blessed in full. The possibilities are endless. You can quote me on that.

Lessons learned while getting up:

1. God Adores You.

2. Grace: Can't Qualify. Can't Disqualify.

3. There's Strength In the Journey.

4. The Difference Between Content and Enough

What lessons did God teach you as you read this chapter?

Today's Date: _____

_____

_____

_____

_____

_____

_____

_____

_____

_____

_____

_____

_____

_____

_____

_____

_____

_____

_____

_____

_____

_____

_____

_____

_____

_____

Chapter 5
Who I Say, I Am

Experience vs. Argument

I heard a quote not too long ago that says, "A man with an experience is never at the mercy of a man with an argument." I've done some research on the Internet to try and find its source to no avail. Despite not being able to locate its source, I am a living testimony of its truth. No matter what anyone else may try to tell me is true about me, what I've actually experienced with God on my own trumps their most persuasive attempts.

This lesson I learned has been debated in theological circles a number of times. Having grown up a Southern Baptist, I probably wouldn't have believed it myself had I not experienced it first-hand. I say these things because I know that I am going into waters where your feet won't touch bottom. These waters will probably feel uncertain and, as one may be in the murky oceans surrounding the United States, you might find them a bit scary not being able to see clearly below the surface. If, however, you grew up in a charismatic church environment, this chapter may be a place of warmth reminding you a little of home.

That being said, I'm going to make claims in this chapter that you may not be able to comprehend. But to play off the quote from the opening statement, I am a man with an experience and not at the mercy of anyone with only an argument. You can try and claim that what I have experienced is only coincidence or even some kind of luck, but I say it has been the work of a holy God in my life revealing His true nature to me as His child.

Name It, Claim It

Let me first make a statement that is my belief as I write this book. I do not believe, based on my current interpretation of scripture, in any kind of "name it, claim it" theology. I don't believe that God responds to us walking into our driveway, laying our hands on the cement, and claiming that a Mercedes will one day fill that spot. I believe God is a God of provision, not indulgence born through selfish greed. We've already spoken about greed. For the vast majority of us, our financial stability is greatly determined by our discipline and obedience when it comes to how we handle our finances. If you are not financially disciplined in your spending, I would not expect an outpouring of blessing in that regard. That's just my opinion based on my interpretation of scripture. God is not into wasting things. He would just be pouring money down the drain if He rewarded a lack of discipline.

When the Bible speaks of prosperity, I believe it to not necessarily be talking about a promise of being millionaires monetarily, but being at a point where all your needs are met through God's provision in our lives. I believe this to be referring to a position where one is not bound by debt, worry, or stress due to finances. God never intended for us to worry. That's quite clear in scripture. So worrying about paying the bills and where the money for the next meal will come from goes against God's plan for our lives as His children.

However, we have the ability in our sinful natures to step outside God's provision for our lives and develop *un*holy discontent. We have discussed that previously as well. And when we do that, we buy things we can't afford, run up debt that will cost us dearly in interest over the course of years to come, and summarily put ourselves in a position to call on God to dig us out of our financial holes. God does not respond to this kind of undisciplined action with favor as it was born out of sinful greed.

It seems that sometimes we give God more credit than what He deserves, normally for things that He would not ordain according to His character outlined in scripture. We see a *huge* house that makes us drool. So we say to ourselves, "I know it's God's will for me to have that house. I *claim* that house in Jesus' name. Now if my loan goes through, I know that will be His confirmation that He wants me to have it."

As Americans, one of the reasons we have seen economic slumps is because banks were giving loans to people who could only afford to pay the interest on a home. The banks *knew* these borrowers had no chance of ever paying back the principal on the loan, yet they granted the loans anyway. I'm not saying that the responsibility fell fully on banks for the loss and foreclosures of homes. What I am saying is that greed took over the minds of people who went for loans that they knew to be much too big for their finances to facilitate. They gambled and they lost big time.

I wonder how many people have been foreclosed on because they believed it was God's will for them to own that home simply because the loan went through? God's will is *never* for us to be in a situation where we are beyond our ability to pay. He doesn't want us to even be in debt. And then, being the Godly people we are (said with a wink), we go to Him and have the audacity to cry out, "HELP!" I can't help but believe that God wants to loosely quote Dr. Phil at that point and look at us and say, "What in the *heck* were you thinking?"

According to scripture we have the power to command mountains to move with only the faith of a mustard seed. I believe that God has established certain laws that have to be obeyed before there is that kind of a response, however. Liken it to someone commanding gravity to cease so that we could all float around. We know that such things are possible with God. In Joshua 10:12, God made the sun to stand still in response to the prayer of Joshua. But Joshua's prayer was not to promote himself as a commanding leader. His heart and his goal were in seeing victory for God's chosen people, the Israelites. And without God's intervention, it could not have happened. It was for the good of the *bigger picture*. The ultimate purpose was for the glory of God. That should be our ultimate purpose as well when making such requests. If not, our purpose proves to be born of selfish greed, which is always sin and never blessed by God.

The Bigger Picture

My intention has not been to paint God into such a narrow corner that a determination is made that nothing that we could speak is within the lawful boundaries He has established in order for the particles of the universe to respond. Quite the contrary. My purpose has been to open your minds and hearts to the very heart and nature of our Heavenly Father and show you the potential of the power He has granted us. Everything boils down to the spiritual condition of our hearts. If we pull away all the fluff, what is the true nature of our desires -- our prayers?

My experience has been that when I speak out loud, if indeed I am speaking things into being that will ultimately be for the good of others while bringing God the glory, then *that* is when I see the "mountains move." It is when my actions are filled with grace, mercy, service, ministry, etc. that God responds to the point of overflowing. Why? Because those things are at the center of His heart. We, and the very atoms and particles that make up the smallest parts of His creation, are both designed to work in unity in accordance with His heart and will. When those two join together, it is truly an unstoppable force. It's a beautiful deeper picture of the relationship we have with Christ. Our relationship is not just personal, like that we would have with a friend, but a spiritual one as well—one where we know what He is thinking and why so that we are acting on His behalf.

I've mentioned Jamie challenging me to draft a five-year plan for myself. As I sat there and prayed, the vision that God gave me was for bringing hope to a hopeless world. As a songwriter, I do my best to build some kind of hope into songs that I write, not that hope is a theme necessarily, but that it definitely brightens the day or touches the heart. As a photographer, I love seeing my subjects' faces light up as they see themselves in my images. Some even shed tears. As an author, I wanted you to know this story and to know that there is hope for you, no matter what you've done or where you've been. As a personal coach/mentor to others, my desire is to speak wisdom into their lives to help them avoid the potholes that have wrecked my life in the past. Other parts of the plan were monetary that included giving money to people in need, to my church, and to charities for whose visions I have a passion. In short, I have asked to be blessed so that I can do things that are much bigger than me. My desire is for my influence— for this message of hope—to reach further than just my immediate sphere of influence. I want my sphere to be the *whole world.*

When my plan was written, I sat back and laughed. Literally. I knew that anyone else who saw such an overwhelming long shot of a plan would have the same reaction and think me to be suffering from severe delusions of grandeur. I even went so far as to start apologizing to God for being selfish and greedy even though I honestly wanted to have success as a songwriter, photographer, and author to be a voice of hope to others.

Yet it was what it was. It was the vision that I believed God had given me for my life. I fired it off to Jamie as he had requested, by 8:00 PM. And I'll never forget his response via email, "Now *that's* a five-year plan with vision!"

We met again not long after I sent my plan. I told him my doubts. He told me he would send me a list of some things that he read out loud daily. These would be things that were simply confessions taken straight from scripture stating who we are in Christ. He challenged me to start reading them *out loud* every day and see if God wouldn't respond.

I've added a couple of things to the list and taken some language from different translations of the Bible so that as I read, each statement makes sense to me, but what you see below is the list that he gave me. The statements are conversational. I want you to have these. And right now, I am challenging you to do as Jamie challenged me. Copy these into a document that you can print and put on your bathroom mirror and say them **out loud** every morning. Saying them out loud is important. Don't miss this simple exercise to watch God's power work in your life.

CONFESS WHO YOU ARE IN CHRIST

• I am strong in the Lord and in His great power. I draw my strength from His boundless wealth of strength. (Ephesians 6:10)

• I am strengthened with His glorious power so that I have all the endurance and patience I need. For I can do all things through Christ who strengthens me. (Colossians 1:11, Philippians 4:13)

- The same spirit that raised Christ from the dead now lives in me and gives life to my mortal body. (Romans 8:11)

- My mind is daily being transformed by God's word and is not in bondage to depression, anxiety, worry, and other weapons against my thought processes. On the authority of God's word, I bring my every thought captive to the obedience of Christ. (Romans 12:2, 2 Corinthians 10:5)

- The law of the spirit of life in Christ Jesus has made me free from the law of sin and death. (Romans 8:2)

- I am complete in Christ and the fullness of God dwells in me. And all the treasures of wisdom and knowledge dwell in me through Christ Jesus. (Colossians 2:3, 9-10)

- Wisdom in my heart is like water in a deep well. I am a person of understanding and I draw it out. (Proverbs 20:5)

- I have perfect knowledge of every circumstance and situation in life for the Spirit of Truth dwells in me. (John 16:13)

- I am delivered from the power of darkness. I know the truth and the truth has set me free. Because Jesus has set me free, I am free completely. (John 8:32, 36)

•   Jesus said that whatever I bind on earth is bound in heaven and whatever I loose on earth is loosed in heaven. I now bind the powers of sin, darkness, curses, and evil from every side and loose the blessings of God to flow into my life. I expect to be overtaken by goodness. (Matthew 18:18)

•   The Holy Spirit teaches me all things and brings all things to my memory. I know and remember who I am. I now use my words and my faith to manifest God's highest and best for me. (John 14:6)

I taped these statements to my bathroom mirror. The first morning saying them out loud seemed awkward to me. I had never done this kind of thing before. As I said, coming up in the Southern Baptist denomination, this kind of thing was never taught. Most often it was linked with the "name it, claim it" brand of theology I spoke about earlier. But I pushed through the awkwardness and said them anyway. I noticed that as I repeated them each day, my belief in their validity seemed to rise with each sunrise.

Again, my plan was quite the long shot. I've had friends in the music industry, but because of my past, they weren't that eager to return a phone call. Yet somehow God had given me a plan of doing things that in Nashville, you'd *have* to have friends helping you to get them done. Then on top of that, you'd need to be *really* good. And on top of that, you'd need to be *really* lucky. Seemingly, it would've been easier to have gone and played the lottery and won three days in a row.

That next week, I was sitting on the second row back at my church. Michelle had to work that morning, so I was there alone (not literally, but you catch my drift). My pastor was speaking that morning on fulfilling your purpose. How fitting.

As I sat there, I began to have destructive thoughts. Doubts flooded my mind about the plan that I'd written down. I started feeling overwhelmingly guilty for daring God the way I'd thought I'd done. Apologies and promises of making things right as soon as I could get to a computer were shooting out of me like a geyser.

So I prayed. It went something like this, "I'm so sorry, God! I have made a mockery out of You and the grace You have shown me. I need to be more realistic in my vision and my approach to it. People would laugh at me if they were to see what I've written down. I don't deserve it, and they know it. It goes against everything I know myself to be when I look in the mirror. *But if it was of You*, give me a sign. Let Pastor say *something* that only You and I would know, and I will have my answer." Pastor reached the end of his message with no sign, no revelation. I had my answer.

He began to pray to close out this section of the service. Then right in the middle of his prayer, *he stopped*. It was only for a second. But when he spoke again, he said something very close to this, "And God, I don't know who this is for, but there is someone here this morning who I believe that within the next five years, You will resource in such a way to help others and change the lives of others, that if they were to tell friends and family right now what You're going to do, they would be laughed at." I know we were supposed to be praying and all, but my head shot up and my eyes flew open, and I started almost spinning around seeing if anyone else was looking because that was meant for them and not me. There was nobody else. Only me.

I bowed my head and cried. How do you say "thank you" for that? The same God, who has seen me at my worst, has chosen to bless me with His best. That's grace in action. That's unconditional love. That is "undeserved *favor*." But my friend, I'm not special. The reason I wrote this book was not to tell you about a hope for me and just wish you the best. *This same hope* is *YOURS, too.*

At the time of writing this chapter, it has been right at eleven months since I sat down to pray about this plan with my computer in my lap. I have gone from knowing nobody and not knowing how any of these things could *ever* get done, to seeing doors kicked wide open on every side. Granted, being in the right place at the right time can bring about great things. For me, being here in Nashville can physically put me in some of those right places. *Or,* I can give God the glory for having my back behind the scenes and give Him the praise He rightly deserves. I believe the latter. There are people, Christian people, in my life who still try to explain it away by assuring me it's because I'm simply in this town. If they want to believe that, fine. I know the truth.

I have met songwriting partners with connections to help get some things done on the secular side of my songwriting. To date, I've fulfilled photography contracts with a major record label along with other good opportunities as a merchandise photographer. The songs I have written are reaching the ears of people I would have never thought possible. There are even more new exciting music possibilities moving forward. And the way that this book is coming into being is through being introduced to a New York Times Bestselling author with fifteen books on the list, three having gone to #1. And he agreed to be a mentor to me for my first book—*this* book.

Are you going to sit and tell me that God isn't in all of that? That it's all just coincidence? That I'm just lucky? Maybe all of this would've happened even if I'd never chosen to speak things into my life *out loud* every day. After those statements, I would go so far as to read off my list of goals for the day in line with the plan that God has given me. It works, people. Remember, I'm a man with an experience, not an argument.

Airport Story

In January of 2014, I flew down to sing in a concert at the church my dad pastors in The Villages, Florida. A friend had supplied me with a "buddy ticket." That's a reduced price ticket given to airline employees that they can provide to friends and family. The only caveat is that all of these types of tickets are standby only. If there's an empty seat, you can fly. If not, you have to wait for a flight that does have an empty seat.

I had been supplied with four of the old school cardboard boarding pass size tickets. It appeared that two would be for the trip down and two for the return flight. As I presented all four to the people at the gate kiosk at my home airport in Nashville, they stapled all four together and told me to go to the gate. Passing by the guy scanning the passes at the gate door, he took all four of mine. I remember asking him if I needed any of that to come home and he said, "No."

After the week of rehearsals and concerts, my scheduled flight was to leave Orlando at 6:30 AM. My parents made sure I was at the airport an hour and a half early in order to get through ticketing and security. I checked my bags, and nobody asked me for anything other than my driver's license. They then presented me with a pass in order to have proof of my flight and get through security.

I made it to the gate kiosk, and they asked me for those other two cardboard passes—the same two I had surrendered in Nashville before leaving. I told them that I didn't have them, and they told me that I would not be allowed on the plane. So I tried to explain what had happened...they stapled...guy took them at gate...said no I wouldn't need them...the whole nine yards. But these ladies were relentless and said that their supervisor would be, too. (I had asked if speaking to a supervisor would change things.)

Reaching for my phone in my pocket, I turned to call my friend who had provided me the tickets to see if there was anything he could do on his end. I needed to get home today.

I hadn't taken but two or three steps away from the kiosk when a blonde-haired woman standing with a young girl asked if I was trying to fly "non revenue" (the technical term for a buddy ticket).

"Yes ma'am, I am. But apparently they took the portion of the ticket that I need to return home in Nashville as I was boarding to come down here."

"Well, I may be able to help. My husband is a pilot with the airline. This is my daughter's best friend. She's 12 years old, and we got her buddy tickets to come and visit us for the weekend. Only when we got them, we accidentally got one more than we need. You can have it if you want. It's only good for one leg, so if you're going any further than Nashville..."

I couldn't believe what I was hearing! Neither could the ticket agents at the kiosk when they saw that I'd returned with the necessary documents, and I explained what had just happened. One of them said, "Sir, I hope you know this *never* happens." I smiled. I had prayed that morning for God to get me home to Michelle. She had been sick all week, and I just felt I needed to get home to her. God was doing His thing.

I turned back to the blonde-haired woman and said, "I don't know what you believe about God, but I'm a Christian. I believe that God had you standing there as an answer to my prayer to get home."

She said, "You don't know the half of it. Yes, I, too, am a Christian and I, too, believe it was all His plan." She began to tell me how her daughter's friend was actually supposed to fly out of Tampa Bay that morning. When she had gone online to check the flight manifest and see if there was a good chance of her actually getting to fly due to the standby nature of the ticket, she found out the flight had been *cancelled*.

She called her husband, the pilot, who was on a run out west to ask what she should do. He didn't understand the cancellation saying that their airline never cancelled flights except for inclement weather. It was sunny and 75 degrees in Tampa that day. But for whatever reason that still remains unknown, it was cancelled. So the husband/pilot sent them to Orlando that morning instead.

Come to find out, this was the little 12-year old's first trip flying, and she was going to need to change flights in Nashville. The girl's mother and my new found friend had prayed and asked God to provide someone safe that would help her to find her next gate upon arrival in Nashville, which I agreed to do.

She concluded by saying, "So I believe that God cancelled that flight in Tampa because He knew that we needed you and you needed a ticket."

That's the Way I Want It

I remember in the late 90's, when I was serving a church in Ohio, my pastor there introduced me to the teachings of Dr. John C. Maxwell. Maxwell has written numerous best-selling books on the subject of leadership, with his book *The 21 Irrefutable Laws of Leadership* being one of my favorites to this very day. Back then, Maxwell was Pastor of Skyline Wesleyan Church in San Diego, California, and did a monthly mentoring club via cassette/CD called *The Injoy Life Club*, appropriately named for his company, Injoy. This club sent leadership lessons to church leaders each month along with lesson notes for you to fill in the blanks.

In one of these lessons, Maxwell stated that he had not originally planned on being a pastor, but instead had a degree in counseling. His story goes that he was so excited to be able to help those in need of hope, that he went into his first few counseling sessions with great enthusiasm. But when they would report back to him the next week for the next session and he asked them how things were going, the response was mostly that things were going the same as they had been going in the weeks prior to counseling. Didn't he give good advice? Of course, he did. It was sound and Biblical advice. Was there follow-up? Yes. The issue back then was the same one that exists today. Those people didn't *want* to change. They either loved the drama, or wanted the magic pill that made everything better with one single dose.

They're the people who always find themselves in the middle of some kind of situation. They're mad at someone, or someone else is mad at them. They've been done wrong by a friend (actually, usually a former friend) or there is a crisis type dilemma. One thing is for certain; it is almost *never* their fault. Always quick to point out the faults in others while ignoring their own, they normally have some level of delusion that has blinded them to the real truth of the circumstance. About five minutes of conversation and the negativity starts to boil out, IF it takes that long.

Maybe this even describes you. It described me at one point. One good way to know if you're in this camp is to look at the people who surround you. Proverbs 13:20 (NLT) says, "Walk with the wise and become wise, associate with fools and get in trouble." Birds of a feather flock together. Always have, always will. If they are negative and long faced, chances are great that you're not the one positive person in the bunch. You are who you hang around. So how do we overcome this destructive pattern to our faith and begin moving in the right direction?

1. Speak Biblical truth. This is where 99% of us will do *exactly* nothing. "What difference will saying stuff make?" we ask ourselves. We seem to question the validity of the advice we receive. We will be the ones about whom Dr. Maxwell remembered. We may say that we're going to do it, but then it drops from the priority list quicker than last year's New Year Resolutions. But you have *got* to start speaking **out loud** the things you *want* to be, not the things you think you *are*. The Bible tells us who we are in Christ. That's why I supplied the confessions in Christ statements for you to speak. Use them. They are a wonderful place to start.

2. Speak practical truth. I recently heard of a pastor who challenged the congregation to put the phrase "and that's the way I WANT it!" right after everything they would say about themselves. It teaches you to pay attention to the way you speak. Try it.

"I'm sick...and that's the way I want it!"

"I had a bad day at work...and that's the way I want it!"

"I didn't get that contract...and that's the way I want it!"

If we start speaking about ourselves in the same way God speaks about us and sings over us, we will start to see changes in our lives. There is POWER in our words!

3. Expect goodness. When trouble comes, recognize it for what it is. John 16:33 (NLT) says, "I have told you all this so that you may have peace in me. Here on earth you will have many trials and sorrows. But take heart, because I have overcome the world." Trials aren't an option. We should *expect* goodness, but recognize trouble as just an attack to distract or discourage us. Your biggest breakthroughs are often preceded by your biggest breakdowns. My pastor says, "The size of your challenge is usually an indication of the size of your future." When trials come, that's the time to push through and persevere knowing that there is goodness waiting just beyond what you can presently see. Expect it.

4. Worship in your pain. David did. Psalm 34:3 (NLT) is from a song of David. David just finished pretending to be insane, Abimilech sent him away, and he started exalting the name of Christ. It says, "Come, let us tell of the lord's greatness; let us exalt his name together." Worship does two things in our pain. First, it takes the focus *off* of our pain and puts it *on* Christ. When we focus on other things, we can't focus on present trials. Second, it creates an attitude of hopeful expectation for God to step in and work. These are the ways He responds best. Remember this: "What you magnify will mess you up or lift you up." Are you magnifying Christ, or do your words magnify your problem?

It is said, "Who you are today is only who you've been *saying* you are for the past year." Most people win or lose their battles on the battlefield that's between their ears—their minds. Then that loss or victory seeps down and out their mouths and into existence. What you entertain in your mind will manifest into speech. What you speak manifests into your life and bears great influence on who you are. At least, this has been *my experience*.

Lessons learned while getting up:

1. God Adores You.

2. Grace: Can't Qualify. Can't Disqualify.

3. There's Strength In the Journey.

4. The Difference Between Content and Enough

5. Who I Say, I Am

What lessons did God teach you as you read this chapter?

Today's Date: _____

_____

_____

_____

_____

_____

_____

_____

_____

_____

_____

_____

_____

_____

_____

_____

_____

_____

_____

_____

_____

_____

_____

_____

_____

_____

_____

Chapter 6
Forgiving Is Essential

Before getting into this chapter, I want to make a short disclaimer so that you understand my intent and do not draw a false conclusion based on the opening sections. When I started writing this book, I wanted to tell only enough about my story as was absolutely necessary. This book is the story of God's work in my life; and I have no desire to make it about me.

To properly set the picture of the level of bitterness and anger that I've felt, I have put more detail about my story in this chapter. Make no mistake; I do not blame anyone or anything else for my own sin. I am the sole responsible party. No matter what happened to me or what environment surrounded me, on the authority of scripture, God made a way out of my temptation for me, and I chose not to take it.

The circumstances I'm about to describe, I believe, were a calculated attack on me, and the church in which I worked, by the enemy. I've been transparent with you and told you about my strong desire to not be disliked by anyone. The devil has always played on that and other weaknesses when he has attacked me. This time was no different. He created the perfect storm. I saw the storm coming. I felt the wind tossing me, the sting of the rain on my skin. I knew that moving forward would bring disaster. Yet I chose to do it anyway thinking that I could handle it. I had navigated storms before, some successfully, some not. So I determined to sail into the storm. That would be a critical error.

A Job Offer in Georgia

I had experienced the greatest two years (plus a couple of months) of my ministry career. Michelle and I had been serving the First Christian Church in Decatur, Illinois, and we loved our staff and the people of the church. If there was ever a pastor who genuinely cared for his staff and knew how to treat a staff, it was Pastor Wayne. God had also blessed me with a terrific team of people in the Worship Arts Department that was passionate about worship and doing things with excellence.

So when a church from my home state of Georgia called me, I honestly wasn't that interested. But something that I'd always done, whether it was really the *best* thing to do or not, I would at least entertain a conversation just to see if God was doing something behind the scenes.

This prospective church's pastor and I made arrangements for him to fly to Illinois in order for us to sit down and talk for a while just to see how we would feel afterward. Following that visit, while I liked him and liked what I had heard about his vision, the situation with the church itself didn't feel right. After prayer about the possibilities, Michelle and I both were in agreement that this was not a move we needed to make.

It hadn't been but maybe two days since I'd hung up the phone with the first pastor, and my phone rang again. It was another pastor (who, choosing not to use his real name, I will be referring to as Jim) in the metro Atlanta, Georgia area wanting to talk to me about coming down as the church's worship pastor. I told Jim that I had just hung up the phone with another church on the opposite end of town just a day or two before and really felt that God had given me an answer with them that Decatur was where I needed to stay for now. That was somewhere around August of 2008.

I can't remember exact timelines, but about a month later, I heard from Pastor Jim again. He said that God still had me on his heart and wondered if I'd just have a conversation. As I said before, it was normally my standard protocol to at least talk, but I had gone against what was normal and had shut him down on the first call. However, he had played the God card and said that "God had me on his heart," so I thought I'd better listen. So we talked.

When he heard that I was writing songs for PraiseCharts, he started backpedaling. He said that he didn't want to hire a guy that wasn't committed to the church and was just using the church as a stepping-stone to get to Nashville one day. (I know. Ironic that that's where I ended up isn't it?) But that was not my goal at all. Nashville was not even in a distant thought. As I said before, I was experiencing my greatest years in ministry and wasn't looking to go anywhere. Since Jim had those concerns, we agreed that he should look elsewhere.

Somewhere around the middle to end of October, Pastor Jim called yet again. He told me that God still wouldn't let me off his heart, and he just knew that I was God's man for the job. He had played the God card yet again, so I was inclined to listen...again. As time would progress, I would find his playing of the God card to be quite the normal happenstance.

Over the next couple of months, we carried on conversations about his vision for SouthWay Church (that's not the actual name, but is how I will be referring to it for the sake of the book). I liked most of what I was hearing. There were a couple of things that seemed a little bit of a red flag, but they didn't seem to be that big of a deal.

As time and talks went on, things started shaping up quite nicely. It looked as if Michelle and I would be able to buy a nice brand new home from a builder who was in the church, that we would be getting a substantial enough raise in salary, plus we would be going back home to Georgia and be closer to friends and family. I was looking for the negatives to this possibility and having a hard time finding any whatsoever.

Time came to bring me in and have me lead worship in a service at SouthWay and see if there was indeed a true fit. The time was set for the last weekend of December in 2008. Meetings were set up with key people that I would see while there for them to ask me questions and me to do likewise.

But then on one of our last conversations before going down, Pastor Jim asked something that threw a BIG red flag up. He asked, "So when you come down and if we offer you the job, are you going to take it?" I had *never* been asked that question prior to even stepping foot on church property in all my years of ministry. The question set me back a little.

I said, "I don't know, Jim. Don't you think that would be better answered after I'm there and get a look around and talk to the people?"

"Look, either you're God's man, or you're not," Jim replied. "So are you God's man, or aren't you? If you're not, there's no point in us spending the money to bring you down." I wish I'd told him to save his money, but instead I assured him, "No, I'm God's man." I would live to regret that statement.

2 Years of Hell

I hadn't even finished loading my truck in Illinois when things started going south with Pastor Jim. I noticed a need for him to constantly have me at his beck and call. There were constant texts no matter the time of day. Personal time wasn't respected at all. My years of leadership and my spiritual gift of counseling told me that his was the behavior of someone who was highly insecure and extremely narcissistic. His view of himself and the way he expected others to view him seemed quite elevated. I chose to ignore it all in a hope that I was wrong. I've honestly normally given people the benefit of the doubt in most circumstances.

He had indeed helped us secure our home with the builder in the church. In that purchase, we were able to take part in a government stimulus package that required homeowners to stay in the home for three years upon purchase. Things were so bad so early with Pastor Jim, that I remember Michelle telling me to text him while sitting at the closing table to buy our home and make sure that he wanted us on staff because we were about to make a three-year commitment, and we couldn't turn back. He said yes, that he wanted me to stay.

Pastor Jim filled the next two years and two months with high levels of abuse and unethical treatment. Our entire staff was seemingly treated this way, not just me. I had never seen the likes of it in all my 24 years in ministry. After arriving there and getting my feet a little damp, I started asking questions of my fellow staff. It was very apparent to me that there was an underlying fear to say anything against Pastor Jim. His skill in being a manipulator was unrivaled. The first time I attended a staff meeting, I was almost sickened by the response from my fellow staff members when he walked into the room. I've always respected my pastors as such and submitted to their authority over me. However, I've never put them on a level higher than myself. Pastor Jim seemingly demanded such from others.

During my time questioning my fellow staff members, I learned about the high turnover rate among all staff there. I'd never asked *that* question during the interview process. The church at that time was less than ten years old. I was about the third or fourth worship leader in that amount of time. Student pastors, associate pastors, and especially administrative staff had been just as expendable. Jim went through four administrative assistants in the two years I was there alone. It was as though Pastor Jim had relational ADD. When he got tired of you, he fired you (or dismissed you as a friend) and got someone else that was a little newer with a brighter shine. And that was quite often. He even taught his staff to not have any relationships that weren't intentional. His criteria for any relationship didn't appear to be caring or loving others, instead relationships were seemingly calculated based on what he would gain from the relationship.

As a result, I was put down in front of other staff, including my own assistants. Michelle's love for Jesus was questioned because "all she volunteered to do at the church" was be a greeter, sing in the choir, and participate in the Small Group Ministry. She was holding down a full time job outside the church and really did all that she had time to do and still try to spend time with me as her husband. Jim's was a ridiculous assessment with no foundation. It honestly angered me greatly.

I was told that an hour or two with my wife on any given day was enough and if I needed more than that, then I had a problem and should seek marital counseling. Daily lunches with her (on days when I didn't have a ministry-related lunch appointment) were discouraged citing a need to be in the office for that hour or so. Yet 55-60 hours a week were demanded in the office. Though I was supposed to get Friday and Saturday off every week, there may have been 4 or 5 times I had actually been able to do so because Pastor Jim had me getting supplies or building sermon props that he wouldn't tell me about until the last minute. If I asked that he tell me earlier, my servant's heart was questioned. This kind of thing wasn't sporadic behavior. It happened almost *every* week, sometimes multiple times a week, for two years and two months.

In any other situation, I would have been in the pastor's office defending my wife or my time with her. I didn't do that with Pastor Jim. To this day, I don't know why. He was vocal to me personally about doing what he said or I wouldn't be able to pay for the house he'd helped me secure. As much as it pains me to admit it, I guess I was just intimidated. Manipulators do that to others, though.

I was extremely bitter and angry, and had been for the entire time I'd been there on staff. (There are parts of me that are still sickened even as I write this.) It affected every part of my personality. Friends and family would come and visit and pull Michelle off to the side and ask what was wrong with me. They noticed that I was no longer the person they had always known. My sense of humor had waned. I seemed heavily stressed and preoccupied. On top of everything else, I was secretly in self-destruction mode; self-medicating on my sin of choice.

The executive pastor told me in March 2011, that I was being let go from SouthWay. They would give me severance, but only if I signed a letter saying that I had actually resigned and told nobody any different. That act made me even angrier. It was a lie and was going to mean that I would need to lie to others, or not be able to meet my financial obligations. At the time, however, there was a lot of my life that was a lie. I actually was in no spiritual or emotional position whatsoever to be a worship pastor. Spiraling behind the scenes, secrets existed about which nobody knew. Eight months and a ton of secret sins later, I would have a gun to my head in my bedroom, almost lose Michelle, would lose my best friend of 30 years, and watch as 99% of the rest of my friends in the area where I lived turned their backs and walked away.

I had a few friends who stuck by me and tried to help, but they were all a few states away. Pastor Wayne offered assistance by flying me back to Decatur, as I mentioned earlier in the book. Pastor Darren, with whom I had served under Pastor Wayne, flew me to Texas for Kairos. I had three or four other guys I could call and talk to, maybe, but nobody was making the first step by calling me. Yet my attitude was that if people didn't care enough to call me, I wasn't going to call them either and interfere with their lives. Anger and bitterness had overtaken me. I was throwing myself a self-pity party. I was also secretly screaming for help! I needed someone to tell me I was dead wrong and that things would be hard, but that they would be right beside me walking through it with me. *That* kind of close friend never appeared.

Receive

Someone once described harboring unforgiveness as "drinking poison and waiting on someone else to die." I would sip on this poison day in and day out multiple times a day. Sometimes it was as though I was guzzling it, pouring it down through a funnel. I was in a place I'd been before and swore I'd never return. At the time, the only one I wanted to blame was Pastor Jim. Looking at the storm that had surrounded that relationship and the devastation that had resulted, pointing the finger at him seemed to be blame well placed.

When you lose things, the hardest person to blame is yourself. Ironically, the same is true when it comes to forgiveness. Eventually I had come to the point that I understood fully that I carried sole responsibility for my choices and the circumstances surrounding me. I hadn't stood up to Pastor Jim. I had my priorities all out of whack. I had let my relationship with Christ slide to the bottom of the totem pole. Once we arrive at the truth of rightly placed blame, at the place of stark reality, that we are the ones who are responsible for our own actions, then we also come to the realization of our shame and guilt. We see ourselves for what we have done and the hurt we have caused others. It's what happens when light comes into darkness—when truth comes face to face with sin. It's what happens in the light of holiness. I was now standing in that light.

This is what causes the feeling that I described earlier as a "hidden death." The weight of sin on the heart of a believer is enormous. It's crushing to the spirit. You understand that the fire of a past has ignited and is feeding on you. You will never be the same. Neither will anyone else ever look at you the same again.

While the previous statement is true about never being the same, the fire can be snuffed out. The true fire of your past is only feeding on your inability to forgive yourself. It's the weight of the guilt and the shame that you carry. You look in the mirror and don't like what you see. That's the fire!

It's the same fire that I'm sure was burning the adulterous woman brought before Jesus by the stone-carrying mob. She was married. We know that because the sin was adultery, not fornication. She had a family at home. As she was being brought to Jesus, can you imagine the questions that the fire was searing into her mind?

What will my husband be told about why I died?

Who will take care of my kids?

What kind of shame will I bring on those left behind?

There was no way to forgive herself for the pain she knew was going to come to those whom she loved most. At that moment, she realized that the rush of the forbidden was not worth the price she would have to pay.

But then, completely unexpectedly, Jesus speaks nothing but grace and love to her. Her accusers drop their stones and walk away. And from the only one left in her presence, she finds no condemnation. In the span of just a few moments, she had gone from death to life; from guilt to pardon; from sin to grace.

This process took months for me. Because of God's grace being so evident in my personal relationship with Him, because of the grace and forgiveness that has been shown to me by Michelle, and because of my wife's prayers for me, I was finally able to start accepting forgiveness.

Understand, this may very well be a process more than an event. I can almost guarantee that this would be true. An immediate event is extremely rare. It may take conversations with you and the Lord, or with you and your spouse, or you and someone else with whom you are in relationship. Don't be frustrated with yourself. God isn't! He's just overjoyed to see you finally be able to pick up what He has already laid at your feet: His forgiveness.

Give

It is impossible to give away that which you do not first possess yourself. Forgiving others cannot happen until you have gone through the process of receiving forgiveness. If others are asking for that action from you, it's perfectly fine to say that your desire is to do so, but that you have to work on forgiving yourself first.

When you are ready, however, forgiving others is a key part to your healing. Scripture tells us, "If you forgive those who sin against you, your heavenly Father will forgive you. But if you refuse to forgive others, your Father will not forgive your sins." (Matthew 6:14-15 NLT) God takes this whole forgiveness thing pretty seriously. Paying our sin debt of death is what Jesus did on the cross. He *redeemed* us—bought us back—with His own life so that our debt could be forgiven. Sin still requires death. He just paid the debt. So if He did that for us, and we receive that gift, how *dare* we not forgive others. Forgiveness of others is necessary *even if* they do not forgive you. Even still, how can we ask of someone else that which we are not willing to do ourselves?

I have heard many pastors and theologians, as well as psychologists, even Dr. Phil, talk about forgiveness. Most explain it one of two ways. They will say that it is the releasing of someone else's obligation to pay a debt or make something right with you. Another way I've heard it explained is that forgiveness is you releasing your obligation to hold someone else accountable for an action taken or a debt owed. Both are true.

But they would tell you that it's perfectly fine to stop right there—that you don't ever have to trust them again or have anything to do with them again. That's where I would have to disagree with them. I think there is a lot more to it if we really get down to what I understand the Biblical intention of forgiveness for each other to be. The Bible's entire message has been a story of redemption and restoration. It is the story of mankind's fall into sin and the buy-back—the redemption—of humanity by Jesus so that right relationship could be restored between God and mankind. In other words, everything goes back to the way it was originally intended.

Ephesians 4:32 (NLT) says, "Instead, be kind to each other, tenderhearted, forgiving one another, just *as God through Christ has forgiven you.*" (Emphasis mine)

Scripture goes on to say in Colossians 3:12-13 (NIV), "Therefore, as God's chosen people, holy and dearly loved, clothe yourselves with compassion, kindness, humility, gentleness and patience. Bear with each other and forgive one another if any of you has a grievance against someone. *Forgive as the Lord forgave you.*" (again, emphasis mine)

The Lord brought us back into a *right relationship* with Himself. If we forgive others as God has forgiven us, which is what *both* scripture passages say above, then not only do we release them of their responsibility to make something right with us, but we also restore our relationship to them as it was before the offense. We give what we have received. We give grace— undeserved *favor*.

Now, please understand, I am not saying that if a spouse that you loved was secretly crazy and molesting your kids, that you should just forgive him and put those kids right back in harm's way. You must think about your safety and that of those for whom you are responsible. But neither am I saying that you are absolved of the responsibility to forgive. You ask, "Yeah, but this person was harming my child!" Your sin took the life of God's child. Forgiveness doesn't happen with a huff under the breath. It is a sincere heartfelt desire from you releasing yourself of the responsibility of holding them accountable while seeking a reconciliation of relationship based on their repentance and acceptance of the offer. According to scripture, I believe this is what Christ has called us to exhibit because it is what He has exhibited to us.

Forgiveness is yet another way that we want to do *enough*, but no more. So we go just far enough that we feel like we've gotten the holy wink from the eye of God and a righteous "thumbs up," and then we go on our merry way. Remember in the introduction when I made reference to putting our hands in the dirt at the foot of the cross to the point that the blood of Christ would have to seep down to reach us? This is what I meant. Forgiveness - love - requires us to get our hands dirty.

The disciples didn't like forgiveness either. It was a point of concern for them. Going again to Matthew 18:21-22, Peter inquires of Jesus on the number of times he should forgive someone who sins against him. He asks if sever times are enough. Jesus reply? "No, not seven times, but seventy times seven!" Jesus didn't mean that we could even stop at 490; He was using that figure as a means to instruct them to *always* forgive. "Lose count," is basically what Jesus was saying.

We Christians try to stay too clean. We don't want to forgive the way that I've pointed out here, because that would mean that we have to associate ourselves with sinful people. GOD FORBID! Yet Jesus has *chosen* to associate Himself with *you*. We worry about our reputations and what others may think, when God is calling us to "just love them" like He did us when we were on the floor and hurting. It's just like the enemy to sell us on a bill of goods that is opposite of what God intended. He's made unbelievers think salvation is so difficult, and he's made Christians think that love is too easy and clean. The opposite is true for both.

Look at what Galatians 6:1-3 (NLT) tells us, "Dear brothers and sisters, if another believer is overcome by some sin, you who are godly should gently and humbly help that person back onto the right path. And be careful not to fall into the same temptation yourself. Share each other's burdens, and in this way obey the law of Christ. *If you think you are too important to help someone, you are only fooling yourself. You are not that important.*" (Emphasis mine)

God never says to worry about what others think when it comes to restoration. He tells us right quick that we are "not that important" if we think we're too good to help others. Love was never intended to be easy and clean. The best picture of love is the cross. And there's nothing easy or clean about that.

Love is a daily choice. I used to believe that one couldn't help with whom they fall in love. That's a lie. Of course, you can. You decide every day to love your spouse, your family, your friends, and others with who you are in relationship. Forgiveness is born out of that love. Sure, love deepens the hurt when those we love betray our trust somehow, but it is also the driving force to redeem and restore that relationship. But it requires us to get our hands dirty in the process.

It always hurts the worst when the one who has hurt us is a friend. After all, we loved them. We supported them. We gave them the best we had to give someone else, and they betrayed our trust. They betrayed our love for them. There is a lesson that I have learned from both sides of the friendship relationship. Friends disappoint and hurt each other. It's a matter of the human condition. It's not intentional. But if you leave a friend because they hurt you, then it was all about *you* to begin with. And that was never friendship at all. It was you being a greedy manipulator. The closer two people are in relationship, the dirtier the forgiveness aspect of the relationship has the potential of becoming.

I forgave Pastor Jim. I forgave my best friend of 30 years. I forgave the others who hurt me and walked away from me. I've found freedom in that ability. Michelle and I prayed scripture over the course of a month and asked God to reconcile the relationships of those dearest to us. Every relationship for which we prayed has been reconciled, except one, my best friend. I miss him. It still hurts when I think about it, but I know I hurt him, too, by the decisions I made. I've tried reaching out to no avail. So I've now left it in the hands of God. Maybe one day I'll get a phone call or bump into him somewhere, and we can talk again. Or maybe he'll pick up this book and read it.

Lessons learned while getting up:

1. God Adores You.

2. Grace: Can't Qualify. Can't Disqualify.

3. There's Strength In the Journey.

4. The Difference Between Content and Enough

5. Who I Say, I Am

6. Forgiving Is Essential

What lessons did God teach you as you read this chapter?

Today's Date: _____

_____
_____
_____
_____
_____
_____
_____
_____
_____
_____
_____
_____
_____
_____
_____
_____
_____
_____
_____
_____
_____
_____
_____
_____
_____

Chapter 7
The Mind Is the Door to Your Life

Access

It is said, "The eyes are the window to the soul." I believe the eyes to be more of a key. Our senses register information with the brain. Sight, taste, smell, hearing, and touch all carry specific information that help us to enjoy and be protected within this world we inhabit. But sight is a little special. It seemingly enhances the need to experience any of the other four. The mind is more of a door to your life, and the eyes are the key to that door.

What we see becomes what we want to experience. When we see something appealing, we want it. We want to touch it, taste it, get the full experience. Lust for anything, not just sexual lust, is normally born out of seeing an object or a person and then eventually moving toward actual experience. Every Fall, I want the newest iPhone. I want the biggest screen with the largest amount of memory. I don't get it, but I want it. Why? Because I see it. I see the newest features, the better displays, and the new physical look, and that's what I want.

But there is an additional step, isn't there? There is a bridge that exists between sight and experience. That bridge is *thought*. When we see something that we want to experience, there is a variable amount of time that elapses before what we have observed is translated into a thought. We think about what it will be like to be in that experience. We draw pictures and fantasize putting ourselves in the experience long before actually being there. How will it feel? What will I be able to accomplish once I have it? What will having it do to my credibility, status in life, or self-esteem? Cost is rarely a question that comes first in the list. My experience has been that it is also the least accurate of assessments. I seemingly always forget to factor in something.

The mind is literally where we are tempted. The senses feed information to the mind *about* the sensation of the experience, but the desire *to* experience is born in the mind. The actual motivation to make decisions of obedience or disobedience is plucked after growing in the fertile soil of our thoughts. So if the enemy is going to gain access into our lives, he is going to do so through the door that is our mind.

I can think of four main weapons that the enemy has used regarding my mind. This list is not exhaustive by any means; these are just the top four. I hope this will help you identify attacks when they come. Understand the use of the word *when* in that sentence. It really isn't an *if*; it's a *when*. These four weapons are:

139

- Deception

- Distraction

- Depression

- Destruction

Deception

Scripture describes the enemy as the "master of deceit" (Daniel 8:25), the "father of lies" (John 8:44) and that he disguises himself as an "angel of light" (2 Corinthians 11:14). These three descriptions combine to make our adversary quite dangerous. He thought so highly of his ability to lie and deceive that he actually tried to pull something over on Jesus, Himself. If he is so secure in his ability to try and fool the very Son of God, don't you think his ability to fool *you* is quite probable? We often make the unwise assumption that we are more powerful than the enemy because Jesus lives inside us. Scripture never says that. 1 John 4:4 actually says that He who is in us is greater than he who is in the world. It is Jesus inside us that is greater, not we, ourselves.

The devil used promises of more money, a house, and even a pastor saying that God wouldn't let me off his heart to help persuade me to move away from Decatur. I'd been through almost that *exact* scenario years before and oddly enough, when moving back home to the Atlanta area from another state. I still bought into it and ignored the red flags. In both situations, the enemy threw just enough in of what *could* be God working that I overlooked the red flags that were telling me it *wasn't* God working. I bought into the exact same lie again some fifteen years later.

It's a reality that we all need to keep in the front of our minds. The enemy doesn't throw something at you that is so against the character of God that you can see it coming a mile away. He wraps everything he does in "good" things. He knows well our desire to be good. That's why scripture refers to him disguising himself as an "angel of light." Our adversary, Lucifer, the devil, was the worship leader of heaven. His very name means "son of the morning." Satan isn't some red man with horns and a pitchfork as depicted in most pictures and cartoons. When you face off with him, he will come to you as the most pleasant person you've ever met. He will disguise himself as a good person, even sometimes disguised as a Christian. His language may include Christian catch phrases. He will be very careful, usually, not to let you know his true intent. His goal is to appeal to your senses, what you feel. That's why it is so important to never follow your heart as a rule of thumb.

He doesn't just mess with one person at a time. He is not like God, in that he can be all places at once, but he definitely has a grand scheme. He sees the intimate sides of all of our lives and manipulates us all. Building in interaction between us is all part of his grand scheme. The devil's schemes are very intricate and well planned. That person who tempts you or lies to you or hurts you may indeed be a well-meaning Christian who has a love for the Lord. They have just been lied to or manipulated by the enemy first, to try to influence you. They are a means to an end for him where you are concerned, and vice versa.

The father that told you you'd never be worth anything when you grew up. The husband who consistently reminds you of what needs to be improved about you in order for you to catch his eye. The woman who looked you in the eye and said she'd always love you and be there for you, yet turned and walked out the door to meet someone else while you thought she was working late. The older cousin who molested you and made you feel shame and cheap. The serial killer, the rapist, the thief who stole both your possessions and your peace of mind, the bully at school, the rude boss at work, the pastor who hurt you...

The enemy is using ALL of these people. It was never *their* words or *their* actions. It was that of the one who is only out to steal, kill, and destroy you. That master of deceit, himself, used others to influence you, and he has used people to influence the ones who influenced you. The chain of events could go on and on and on.

It doesn't mean that we can't or shouldn't hold people accountable for their actions. What it *does* mean is that we have been ignoring the reality of our enemy and his work in our lives and the lives of others, that our eyes only see the person who has influenced *us*, and not the one who is influencing *them*. And just because someone says something to you that harms you, doesn't mean that there was any kind of intent to do so. Some of the most hurtful things ever said had the best of intentions behind them.

Dictionary.com defines *deceit* as: concealment or distortion of the truth for the purpose of misleading, duplicity, fraud, or cheating. The mind is the part of us that either sees through the deception, or believes it. Are there instances that the Holy Spirit has brought to your mind as you've read this where you believe you have been deceived by the enemy? You may be able to analyze it from an objective logical point of view and see how God could very well be in it. But remember this, 99.9% real is 100% counterfeit. If it's not perfectly in line with scripture in every way, it's not at all in line with God or His will for you.

Distraction

If the enemy can't deceive you, if you're walking closely with God and our Heavenly Father lets you know the truth about what's up, then he will *distract* you.

Remember my being happy in Illinois? I was at the very peak of what I had dreamed of in ministry. There weren't any plateaus or downgrades in sight. God was using the entire team to not only lead in worship in our church, but to train other worship leaders with resources and tools to help them be better and to better lead the people in their churches in worship. We were taking our gifts outside the walls of the church (little "c") so that we might better be the Church (big "C"). The former denotes the local church I was a part of, the latter being the worldwide global entity encompassing all denominations.

So the devil comes along at a time when I was so close to God, a time when my defenses were up and I could not have been deceived at first, and he distracted me instead. He knew Georgia was home. He knew that my best friend at the time lived there, that my family was still there, and that one of my dreams at some point was to return. The first church didn't do it. So he used another right on the heels of the first. But with this second, he throws in a house, a much bigger salary, and a church with a certain level of prestige within the community.

It didn't take long for me to start looking over at the bait he was dangling with some serious interest. My eyes saw a possibility, and my mind started thinking about that possibility. I started envisioning myself in a new home, getting together with friends and family often, and Michelle and I living in a much less stressed environment. See what I mean? He was using that which was good, something for which I had longed anyway. It wasn't something that I could see coming a mile away. It was *home*. He distracted me with *home*.

Have you ever been to a magic show? A lot of magicians now call themselves what they really are, *illusionists*. David Copperfield never *really* made the Statue of Liberty disappear, but he made it *look* like he had. There's always the unseen mirror, the cloud of smoke, or the hidden keys to make you think you see something that, in actuality, never really happens. Card tricks are done with sleight of hand and "forcing" a certain outcome. We don't know it at the time, but we are actually being played like a Stradivarius. Part of the illusion of a magic show is the desire to be entertained. When we show up, the whole reason we buy a ticket, walk into a room, or move closer to the guy on the street in the middle of the crowd, is that we have a desire to be entertained. We are *expecting* to be amazed. Magicians simply fill our own expectations. It's not until we wonder how a trick happened and start doing some research that we figure out the truth—if we ever do. They keep us looking at the hand or place they need our attention focused on so that they can do something else with the other hand. And we fall for it.

Such are the schemes of our enemy. He knew what my desires were. When I got a phone call from a much larger church, I was *expecting* a bigger salary and more perks. My happiness level rose because I was going to be closer to family and friends. He distracted me with home. I bit for it. I took the bait hook, line, and sinker. In my mind there were just too many positives. God *surely* had to be in it! But what I experienced once I had given in and moved *home* would've never happened at "*home*." It was the equivalent of doing the research after the trick. I saw the mirrors. The smoke faded away. He distracted me, and then laid on the deception that he didn't get me with the first time. I had now been deceived.

The ultimate result when I found I had been tricked was that I came to *resent* home. I realized that I didn't belong there. Not only did I not belong, I *hated* it there. *Home* was no longer home. Day after day it was stacking up with mountains of bad memories and unwise choices. I saw a monster growing inside of me that I didn't like, but had no idea how to rid myself of his presence. I felt trapped. Rascal Flatts said it best, "But I never dreamed home would end up where I don't belong. I'm moving on."[1] Which brings me to the next weapon the enemy used against me.

Depression

I've always been a social person. People matter to me. I guess that's why it matters so much if people like me. Having been known as "the nice guy" for most of my life, having people walk away, especially longtime friends - even my *best* friend - was foreign. It's not that there'd never been anyone who didn't like me or that I'd disappointed, but I'd never seen such a mass exodus as what I was experiencing. I found out that my opinion of myself was based more than I'd ever imagined on what everyone else thought about me. When they were suddenly gone, there was nobody there to fuel what I needed from others. Though technically I wasn't completely alone, I felt alone. Very alone.

Some disagree with the statement, "perception is reality," but that's exactly what it seemed to me. I looked around and didn't see anyone; therefore, in my mind I had been abandoned. Anyone who has ever been alone will tell you, it is the perfect breeding ground for depression. Your mind starts playing tricks on you, and you start believing the headlines that everyone else is writing about you. The devil turns up the heat as well. The pressure of him reminding you how much you've failed God and others haunts you.

Momentum is your best friend or your worst enemy. Even the devil knows that. He uses momentum against mankind daily. The momentum of the enemy in my life had me on a downward spiral that I couldn't control. The weapons of deception and distraction had worked quite well. Depression naturally came next. Thoughts of suicide were almost constant. If the sin doesn't kill you, the consequences just might. Little by little I was wearing down and melting away. Call it a pity party if you want, but it was more than that. It wasn't pouting. It was pain.

I was never without a reason to die. My daily chore was actually finding a reason to *live*. My wife, my family, people I didn't even know, all joined together in prayer for me. Actually, I need *you* to see the last part of that sentence again. *People I didn't even know all joined together in prayer for me.*

Please know that no matter what you see, there are people you don't even know that are praying for you. I thought if I couldn't see them, they didn't exist. That was only another use of deception by the enemy in my life. If you are thinking, as I did, that there isn't anyone who cares about you anymore and you're not worthy of care by someone else, the devil is using the same weaponry against *you*. It wasn't until *afterwards*, that those who had been praying for me started sharing with me what they had done. Only then could I look back and see times I felt alone, but for some reason hadn't given up; I hadn't pulled the trigger. There were times like when Michelle had asked me to go to church; I'd gone even though not really wanting to. Looking back on so many instances on the brink of self-destruction, there had been *something* that had changed my mind that day, that minute, that second, and I'm alive today because of it. It was the prayers of others. There were people praying me through every day. None more so than my wife, Michelle.

There's a song that I've lived. It stands as an encouragement to me to this day. Allen Asbury recorded it. The name of the song is *Somebody's Praying Me Through.* Here are the lyrics:

Pressing over me like a big blue sky

I know someone has me on their heart tonight

That's why I know it's gonna be alright

'Cause somebody's praying me through

Somebody's praying me through

It may be my Mother, it might be my Dad

Or an old friend I've forgotten I had

But whoever it is I'm so glad that

Somebody's praying me through

Somebody's praying me through

Through the tears, through the rain

Through the sorrow, through the pain

It keeps bringing me through

Over and over again

So when you're drowning in a sea of hurt

And it feels like life couldn't get any worse

There's a blessing waiting to push back the curse

'Cause somebody's praying you through

Somebody's praying you through

Someone got down on their knees

And prayed for me

Somebody's praying

Somebody's praying you through[2]

Know this, my friend. If there isn't *one* other person who is praying for you, *I am*. That's something I'm doing even right now as I type these words. I'm praying for every reader who will read these pages that my voice—God's voice through me—would be just the encouragement you need to push through. As I said in the Introduction, "Find in my struggles a strength to inspire you, a trailblazer before you who might help you avoid the traps. Ride on my shoulders for a little while and take a rest. Breathe." I'm praying you through, my friend.

My pastor during the healing stages of 2012, Dave Divine, at the Church at Chapel Hill in Douglasville, Georgia, is a wise and gentle man who carries the heart of a servant. In a recent message that I was viewing online, Pastor Dave says this, "Worry undealt with leads to anxiety. Anxiety undealt with leads to depression. Depression undealt with leads to suicidal thoughts." I would add that suicidal thoughts undealt with lead to our next weapon, the ultimate goal of our enemy.

Destruction

The bigger your purpose, the bigger your problems. Our enemy is on an all-out attack on your life to destroy you. He knows your potential, and whatever that potential is determines the type and the magnitude of the assault he uses against you. In light of that statement, how many of you are looking at your life and wishing your purpose wasn't so great? (Ha!)

The adversary basically has only two ultimate options when it comes to your destruction. He can deceive you and distract you from believing in what Jesus did for you on the cross in paying your sin debt of death and redeeming you - buying you back - into a right relationship with God, or he can destroy your will and your ability to do anything great while you're on this earth. For me, as a believer in Jesus, his only option was the latter.

Satan made me think that I no longer had a purpose. Then he convinced me that a person with no purpose should be no person at all. Suicide became my answer. I saw no other way. But God knew a way. God knew about *you* too and about your circumstances. He knew that when the time was right that I would pick up my computer and start telling this story for those who would come behind me. God knew that He could get glory from my life because I would share what He's done in me and, in turn, give hope to others. God wants you to know that there's hope.

My purpose was never destroyed or taken away. The adversary had merely used some effective smoke and mirrors to hide it from me. It was the same as a large-scale card trick. He had me looking in the direction he determined rather than looking toward Jesus and seeing a hope in spite of who I was or what I'd done.

God wasn't *withholding* anything from me, He was *preparing* me. Those are two completely different things. Rick Godwin says, "Delay isn't denial. It's a chance for your character to catch up with your calling." My character was only catching up with that to which God had purposed me. My purpose wasn't gone at all.

Once you live in a certain spot for so long, no matter how uncomfortable or foreign it may have been at arrival, you come to think of it as home. I'd had memories of Georgia growing up. Even though I'd moved around a lot during the first part of my life, Georgia was always *home*. But when I went back, it seemed foreign and uncomfortable. When the smoke and mirrors rolled away and I saw the wizard behind the curtain, there was nothing left there that I had remembered or would liken to anything of being called home. So the enemy started trying to convince me that I'd been wrong about *home* all along. That there had actually never been any such thing.

In actuality, what I'd been wrong about was what I looked to as *being* home. I had a false definition of home. Georgia wasn't home. Tennessee isn't home either. Even though my parents are there and I love the people at their church, Florida isn't home either. My home is with my Heavenly Father. Jesus said, "Do not let your hearts be troubled. You believe in God; believe also in me. My Father's house has many rooms; if that were not so, would I have told you that I am going there to prepare a place for you? And if I go and prepare a place for you, I will come back and take you to be with me that you also may be where I am." (John 14:1-3 NIV) I know that there is a purpose for me that still needs to be fulfilled first, but I still think about home - my *real* home.

Overcoming the Enemy

You need to decide *right now* what is okay with you. Is it okay to be lied to by the enemy? Is it okay to accept who he says you are rather than who God says you are?

Is it okay with you to be depressed; not believing you have a purpose and that God has declared you unusable? If the answer to any of these questions is "yes," then close the book because you're done reading anything here that will help you. But if the answer is "no," and you are willing to determine this within your heart, read on. Hope lies ahead.

In leadership circles, it is often said "your attitude determines your altitude." I've never met one successful person yet who views themselves as being *un*successful. Or maybe you think attitude doesn't matter to God, that it puts glory on the person, not on Christ. Tell me then, why do you think God put Romans 8 (NIV) in the Bible? It is nothing but a pep talk. I want you to see it in its entirety.

1Therefore, there is now no condemnation for those who are in Christ Jesus, 2because through Christ Jesus the law of the Spirit who gives life has set you free from the law of sin and death. 3For what the law was powerless to do because it was weakened by the flesh, God did by sending his own Son in the likeness of sinful flesh to be a sin offering. And so he condemned sin in the flesh, 4in order that the righteous requirement of the law might be fully met in us, who do not live according to the flesh but according to the Spirit. 5Those who live according to the flesh have their minds set on what the flesh desires; but those who live in accordance with the Spirit have their minds set on what the Spirit desires. 6The mind governed by the flesh is death, but the mind governed by the Spirit is life and peace. 7The mind governed by the flesh is hostile to God; it does not submit to God's law, nor can it do so. 8Those who are in the realm of the flesh cannot please God. 9You, however, are not in the realm of the flesh but are in the realm of the Spirit, if indeed the Spirit of God lives in you. And if anyone does not have the Spirit of Christ, they do not belong to Christ. 10But if Christ is in you, then even though your body is subject to death because of sin, the Spirit gives life because of righteousness. 11And if the Spirit of him who raised Jesus from the dead is living in you, he who raised Christ from the dead will also give life to your mortal bodies because of his Spirit who lives in you. 12Therefore, brothers and sisters, we have an obligation—but it is not to the flesh, to live according to it. 13For if you live according to the flesh, you will die; but if by the Spirit you put to death the misdeeds of the body, you will live. 14For those who are led by the Spirit of God are the children of God. 15The Spirit you received does not make you slaves, so that you live in fear again; rather, the Spirit you received brought about your adoption to sonship. And by him we cry, "Abba, Father." 16The Spirit himself testifies with our spirit that we are God's children. 17Now if we are children, then we are heirs—heirs of God and co-heirs with Christ, if indeed we share in his sufferings in order that we may also share in his glory. 18I consider that our present sufferings are not worth comparing with the glory that will be revealed in us. 19For the creation waits in eager expectation for the children of God to be revealed. 20For the creation was subjected to frustration, not by its own choice, but by the will of the one who subjected it, in hope 21that the creation itself will be liberated from its bondage to decay and brought into the freedom and glory of the children of God. 22We know that the whole creation has been groaning as in the pains of childbirth right up to the present time. 23Not only so, but we ourselves, who have the firstfruits of the Spirit, groan inwardly as we wait eagerly for our adoption to sonship, the redemption of our bodies. 24For in this hope we were saved. But hope that is seen is no hope at all. Who hopes for what they already have? 25But if we hope for what we do not yet have, we wait for it patiently. 26In the same way, the Spirit helps us in our weakness. We do not know what we ought to pray for, but the Spirit himself intercedes for us through wordless groans. 27And he who searches our hearts knows the mind of the Spirit, because the Spirit intercedes for God's people in accordance with the will of God. 28And we know that in all things God works for the good of those who love him, who have been called according to his purpose. 29For those God foreknew he also predestined to be conformed to the image of his Son, that he might be the firstborn among many brothers and sisters. 30And those he predestined, he also called; those he called, he also justified; those he justified, he also glorified. 31What, then, shall we say in response to these things? If God is for us, who can be against us? 32He who did not spare his own Son, but gave him up for us all—how will he not also, along with him, graciously give us all things? 33Who will bring any charge against those whom God has chosen? It is God who justifies. 34Who then is the one who condemns? No one. Christ Jesus who died—more than that, who was raised to life—is at the right hand of God and is also interceding for us. 35Who shall separate us from the love of Christ? Shall trouble or hardship or persecution or famine or nakedness or danger or sword? 36As it is written:

"For your sake we face death all day long; we are considered as sheep to be slaughtered."

37No, in all these things we are more than conquerors through him who loved us. 38For I am convinced that neither death nor life, neither angels nor demons, neither the present nor the future, nor any powers, 39neither height nor depth, nor anything else in all creation, will be able to separate us from the love of God that is in Christ Jesus our Lord.

So in overcoming the enemy, if Step 1 is deciding what is okay with you, Step 2 should be to KNOW WHO YOU ARE. Don't be lied to! If you are in Christ (in other words, you believe in Him and accept His gift to you on the cross), then this is what *scripture* says about you:

- You are not condemned. (vs. 1)

- You are *alive* because of righteousness. (vs. 10)

- You are a child of God. (vs. 14)

- You are a son/daughter of God. (vs. 15)

- You are an heir of God, an actual co-heir with Christ. (vs. 17)

- You possess the firstfruits - the best - of the Holy Spirit. (vs. 23)

- You have the help of the Holy Spirit praying for you in your weaknesses. (vs. 26-27)

- You have the assurance that all things are working together for your good and that you are called according to the purpose of God. (vs. 28)

- You are predestined, called, justified, and glorified by God. (vs. 30)

- You have God on your side. (vs. 31)

- You have Jesus Christ, Himself, interceding on your behalf. (vs. 34)

- You are more than a conqueror! (vs. 37)

- You are unable to be separated from the love of God that is in Christ Jesus! (vs. 39)

And these things that are listed here are just from Romans 8 alone. The Bible is an entire love letter to *you* from your Heavenly Father. He wants you to know Him and how He sees you through His eyes, not the eyes of others.

Do you remember the moment you were born? Of course not! That was a long time ago. We didn't *choose* to forget that moment, we just *can't* remember. However, God can will Himself to forget. We cannot. The only way mankind has of forgetting is through the replacing of information. We cannot remember the moment of birth because too many things have happened since then and the information hasn't gotten buried. It's still there, we just can't recall it. That brings us to Step 3 in overcoming the enemy.

1. Determine what is okay with you

2. Know who you are

3. Read *daily* from God's word

The things that God did for us yesterday, while great and awesome, won't be good enough for what next week might bring. God wants us to rely on Him every day. That's why, with the only exception being salvation, He doesn't just appear to our rescue one time and then we're on our own from there. Our Heavenly Father desires *relationship* with us. Your salvation - the moment you believed on Jesus for your sin debt and decided to follow Him for the rest of your life - was merely the introduction. What happens from then on is the relationship.

In Hebrews 4:12, the Bible describes itself as "alive and active." I have found that to be oh so true. Verses that I have read a thousand times seem to morph to match today's issues as I read them again; almost as if I was reading them for the very first time. Brand new insights are born before my eyes and apply just how I need them to with impeccable timing. I find that as I read, God will bring to memory moments when He has come through for me or spoken to me in times past. Those reminders strengthen me for the task at hand, or for tomorrow's challenges. I'm able to face them with confidence knowing that I'm more than a conqueror in Jesus.

These are things that God brings back to my *mind*. He knows that there is a constant war for the space between my ears, and He wants me to stay in close relationship to Him so that I can discern His voice from that of the enemy. Once again, it's like the shepherd who holds the sheep to his chest so that the sheep hears the shepherd's heart. God wants me to hear His heart and know that it is beating for me because He loves me.

My sin stopped His heart. His love for me made it beat again.

Step 4 is to choose your friends carefully. "Birds of a feather flock together." Remember? If you look around you and wonder why you have negative and sour friends, chances are really good that *you* are negative and sour too. Maybe you don't have friends like that because the birds you've been hanging out with are buzzards and not eagles. Change your environment. Get to places where eagles hang out. Eagles will not come to hang with a buzzard and try to motivate the buzzard to fly higher. It's not in a buzzard's DNA to fly that high. It will be *you* that has to make the move. Remember, *attitude determines altitude.* Be positive and get with positive people.

Before moving on, let's review our steps to overcoming the enemy:

1. Determine what is okay with you

2. Know who you are

3. Read *daily* from God's word

And...

4. Be accountable to someone of the same sex, or your spouse

I would suggest to you that someone of the same sex is best. There are things that, as a man, I will discuss more openly with another man than I would my wife. Why? Because men have different issues than women in many matters. The same is true for women. You will tell a girlfriend things that you might not want to tell your husband; like how much you just spent at the store on your shoes. The person you let into the most intimate details of your life needs to be someone that you trust and that with which a mutual trust is also displayed.

But knowing that, if you're married, a spouse may be the most available person to you without having to go back to hanging out with buzzards. If indeed your spouse is an eagle, then choose to be accountable to that person. The person to whom you're accountable should be someone who is for *you* in every way. Not someone who just happens to like the same kinds of movies you do, or shops at the same stores as you, or walks their dog at the same time you walk yours. These need to be tested people who you *know* have your best interests at heart. They need to have permission to ask you *any* question they want to ask you about *anything* they feel necessary. And they need to DO THAT!

You may not have *anyone* in your life like that right now. And you need to know that's okay. As you make a run through the relationships you currently have, or as you go out into new environments and start meeting some eagles, have your radar up and going about who might potentially fill that role. Don't rush the process. Remember from our previous chapter that the process is where you learn and grow and gain information. Let it happen with patience and prayer. It may be that the only person you need to be accountable to at the moment is God. Maybe you just need to let Him love you. That was my experience. I'm only now in the process of building these tested kinds of relationships with others. My goal in that regard hasn't been reached either.

There will need to be some personal accountability with yourself - with your character - in this process. You are going to need to determine within yourself that you will be truthful when asked the questions by your accountability partner. If you will try to lie to yourself and God, you will lie to others. That's why this person needs to know you quite well. They need to know your patterns and the way you think. They need to be able to discern if you are being truthful in your answers.

I have included some verses in the back of the book in Appendix B on the subject of the mind. Take some time to read these. Maybe you even want to memorize one a week.

A sight becomes a thought.

A thought becomes an action.

An action becomes a habit.

Your mind is indeed a door. What you let in doesn't determine your purpose, but it *does* determine your potential. God's word will change you and equip you. It will strengthen you today by reminding you of yesterday and giving you promise for tomorrow. Let the word of God stand watch at the door of your mind and see for yourself that if He is for you, who can be against you?

Side Note: The chapter you've just read has been the absolute MOST difficult for me to write. Believe me, it's not because of a lack of experience in dealing with the enemy! I have been under attack since writing the first word of the book, but especially this chapter. The adversary has done his best to distract me, scramble thoughts, cloud my mind, tempt me, anything in his arsenal has been fired that may prevent me from being effective in letting you know about the hope that is available to you. But my prayer is that this has found its mark in the core of your heart. I pray God has spoken to you and that you have seen yourself for who you are in Christ instead of who the devil will try to remind you that you have BEEN. Remember, I'm praying for you.

Lessons learned while getting up:

1. God Adores You.

2. Grace: Can't Qualify. Can't Disqualify.

3. There's Strength In the Journey.

4. The Difference Between Content and Enough

5. Who I Say, I Am

6. Forgiving Is Essential

7. The Mind Is the Door to Your Life

What lessons did God teach you as you read this chapter?

Today's Date: _____

_____
_____
_____
_____
_____
_____
_____
_____
_____
_____
_____
_____
_____
_____
_____
_____
_____
_____
_____
_____
_____
_____
_____
_____
_____

Chapter 8
A Changed Life Brings A Changed Perspective

Forward Fixed

I heard it said recently, "Don't let your future be determined by the people in your past." I wrote those words down in my notes and starred them. I felt they had been spoken directly to me. After all, I'm the guy that cared too much what others thought about me, and I let that determine what I thought about myself; my identity.

Now, however, others' thoughts about me no longer define me. It's not because I no longer care. Quite the contrary! It's only because I have made the choice to believe what God says about me. It's a choice made not just daily, but moment by moment. It's not easy. Maybe over time it will get easier, but that time is not here yet.

There are plenty of people who are still talking about me and reminding me of my failures. They're waiting on me to fail again. To them, I am defined by my mistakes. And you know, I've had to come to the place that I have to be okay with however they choose to define me. After all, I made those mistakes. It doesn't mean that I agree with them; I don't. They simply have the right to their own opinion. I've had to accept that there's no way to confirm the change that has taken place in me. There's no way I can sit down and lay out all that God has taught me and is doing in me right now. What good would it do? None. They will still think what they want to think.

All the way back in Chapter 3, we started out by talking about how we have to begin with truth. We have to know who we are and where we are. As for where you are, I pray that you're in a better place than you were at the beginning of this book. I pray that you see the fact that no matter where you are, *you don't have to stay there.* As for who you are, if you believe in Jesus, I'm just going to stand on the word of God and refer you back to Romans 8 from our last chapter. If you need to, read that chapter daily just as a simple reminder. Let the words of our Heavenly Father speak into you and drown out the opinions of others.

If you know those two things about yourself, you're already a changed person. You can look at yourself in the mirror with some dignity and once again dream dreams and realize Godly visions about your life. Feel with every ounce of your being those things for which you are passionate. For your *passion* leads to your *purpose* which leads to your *promise.*

I don't want to make light of the negative things people will say about you. One of the biggest lies out of hell is that "sticks and stones may break my bones, but words will never hurt me." Words hurt! They cut! They assassinate the character and the self-esteem. We, however, can determine the depth of the wound. Remember my desire to please those in authority over me? It didn't matter if they spoke truth about me or not. I gave more weight to what they said because of who they were and so the wounds cut deeper.

We need to rightly assess the person to whom we give the most weight. Maybe we even have a list. Of course it should start with God and what He says about us. Others who should carry weight may include spouses, parents, siblings, mentors, etc. These are people who are not just for what you're for, they are for *you*.

So let our "fan clubs" say what they want to say behind our backs. Let them try to remind us of our pasts. I don't know about you, but I'm going to be like Paul who said in Philippians 3:13-14 (NLT), "No, dear brothers and sisters, I have not achieved it, but I focus on this one thing: Forgetting the past and looking forward to what lies ahead, I press on to reach the end of the race and receive the heavenly prize for which God, through Christ Jesus, is calling us." *That* is the promise that will result from my passion and purpose.

Face forward. Push ahead. Let them say what they will, but do not be deterred. Steve Maraboli said, "If people refuse to look at you in a new light and they can only see you for what you were, only see you for the mistakes you've made, if they don't realize that you are not your mistakes, then they have to go." Let them go.

What's My Name?

Any company that has survived years of building a brand around a name will tell you, names matter. There is a lot riding on a name. Reputations, lawsuits, promotions, guilt, and innocence can all ride on a name. One of the first responsibilities ever given to man by God after creation was naming the animals. God gave Adam and Eve their names. Your parents probably named most of you. Names count. They matter. People, organizations, even nations all respond to a name.

As I look through and read scripture, I see this fact drilled home as I see those whose names were changed after significant events in their lives. Here's a short non-exhaustive list:

Jacob - "What is your name?" the man asked. He replied, "Jacob." "Your name will no longer be Jacob," the man told him. "From now on you will be called

Israel, because you have fought with God and with men and have won." (Genesis 32:27-28 NLT)

Paul - Saul, also known as Paul, was filled with the Holy Spirit, and he looked the sorcerer in the eye. (Acts 13:9 NLT)

Abraham - When Abram was ninety-nine years old, the lord appeared to him and said, "I am El-Shaddai—'God Almighty.' Serve me faithfully and live a blameless life. I will make a covenant with you, by which I will guarantee to give you countless descendants." At this, Abram fell face down on the ground. Then God said to him, "This is my covenant with you: I will make you the father of a multitude of nations! What's more, I am changing your name. It will no longer be Abram. Instead, you will be called Abraham, for you will be the father of many nations. (Genesis 17:1-5 NLT)

Gideon - But Joash shouted to the mob that confronted him, "Why are you defending Baal? Will you argue his case? Whoever pleads his case will be put to death by morning! If Baal truly is a god, let him defend himself and destroy the one who broke down his altar!" From then on Gideon was called Jerub-baal, which means "Let Baal defend himself," because he broke down Baal's altar. (Judges 6:31-32 NLT)

Each of these men had something significant happen in their lives, and their names were changed as a result. Their new names reflected the events or circumstances for which they would be known.

Gideon was the last name I listed above. I recently did a study on the few chapters in Judges that record for us the life of Gideon. There's not much there, but what is there is powerful.

He was raised in a society that worshipped an idol named Baal. There was an altar to Baal in Gideon's parents' home where he had grown up. As a matter of fact, Gideon's first act of obedience to Jehovah God was to go to the home of his father and tear down the altar of Baal. The verses above pick up right after this event. We see the people calling for Gideon's life. Yet the name that he ended up getting was one that meant, "let Baal contend for himself." Basically, "Baal Fighter."

Upon reading this story, I began to think about my passion and my purpose to which I am called. I look at the ways God has gifted me and am trying my best to understand how to use these gifts most effectively to make differences in the lives of those around me. So I wondered, what would *my* name be? If God were to call me by a name that He would give me based on who I am in His eyes and my purpose, what name would that be?

Those of you who know me personally call me, *Kevin*. It is how I am known and the name to which I respond. But I believe with all my heart that I have another name. I believe it may even be the name referenced in Isaiah 43 (and surrounding chapters) when the scriptures continually remind us that God has "called you by name." (Isaiah 43:1) "I have called you by name and you are mine." This passage tells us that when waters overcome us, we won't drown; when we find ourselves in the fire, we won't be burned up. Maybe, just maybe, the name that He calls out is one that defines us as He sees us. Maybe this name has the power of His might standing behind it. Could it be that God speaks our name in return to us speaking His and the waters recede, the fires fall back, the mountains crumble, and the ways are made straight?

In Revelation 2, we see the letter to the Church in Pergamum. At the end of this brief letter, we read in Revelation 2:17 (NLT), "Anyone with ears to hear must listen to the Spirit and understand what he is saying to the churches. To everyone who is victorious I will give some of the manna that has been hidden away in heaven. And I will give to each one a white stone, and on the stone will be engraved a new name that no one understands except the one who receives it."

Does this mean that all of us who claim the name of Christ, who have placed our faith and trust in Him as Savior, who devote our lives in the pursuit of holiness have received a "new name" that only we will understand? I think it just might.

So if our God-given names represent who we are while here on this earth and the great things we do for the cause of Christ, what do you want your name to be? When you walk through the gates of heaven and you look your Savior in the face for the very first time, and He says, "Welcome home, _____," take a moment and fill in that blank. What is it that you want your life to stand for? When you wrote out your obituary and epitaph, what name would reflect your desire for the way you finish this life?

I'm afraid for so many of us, we may be trying to leave Jesus at a loss for words because we're not doing much of anything to earn a name greater than "Warmer of Many Seats." This thing I know about all of us who claim the name of Christ, we are the body of Christ, according to scripture. All of us have different gifts, different roles within the body. There's no part of the body of Christ that is paralyzed. We are to be active by definition. And within this activity, there is no retirement plan in this life. We don't quit changing lives because we get older. Heaven forbid! With age comes wisdom. Those who come behind us will rely on our wisdom. We can show others where the potholes are on this journey of life. We can still help those younger than us navigate their way to the finish line possibly with fewer scars than we accrued along the way. A spectator never scores a point and the Holy Spirit already fills the role of the referee. So everyone is in the game. We're all called to do our jobs on the team. So what name do you want on the back of your jersey?

For me? *Messenger of Hope*, or *Hope Bringer*. That's not a very pretty name in English, but it really is how I want to be remembered. Whatever my name is that is waiting for me, aside from seeing Jesus, it'll be the best moment of the beginning of my eternity...when I get to hear my name for the first time. Imagine that moment for you for just a minute. We enter the stadium where we have been cheered on by that "great cloud of witnesses" spoken of in Hebrews 12:1. As we enter, we hear Jesus call us by our name as having finished the race. The crowd erupts in cheers as those loved ones who have gone before us hug our necks and usher us to see our Lord face to face for the first time. Can you see it?

Your life has changed. Your past has passed. Those who only identified you based on past sins and failures are going to start blurting out, constantly reminding you of your past for which they knew you. But God will be cheering you on; calling out the name that He has for you that is so intimate only you can understand it. W.C. Fields once said, "It's not what people call you, it's what you answer to." Determine now. What name will you answer to? Your past? Or your future?

A New Perspective

Not only has your life changed, but you're now going to see the world around you a bit differently. Bishop T.D. Jakes writes, "A turtle and a giraffe can occupy the same space at the same time, but they're going to have a different world view." Your worldview is going to be quite different than before. I'm not talking about the way you see yourself and your circumstances, but the way you see others.

You will find that your compassion has increased. There will be those with whom you come in contact who either are, or have been, going through circumstances very similar to those surrounding your life experiences. And just as you were when you were on the floor, they will be looking for someone to listen and share their hurt. You remember those days from your time on the floor, right? I know I do. I pray we never forget them.

They may have just lost their lifetime best friend. They do not need you to try and *replace* that friend. You couldn't even if they wanted you to. But you see the look in their eye and you recognize it. It's all too familiar to you. It's a look of hopelessness that they try to hide and don't know the indelible ink with which it is written on their face.

You don't need to know the right words to say. As a matter of fact, you *won't* know the right words to say.

Just listen. Be a person of grace. Be a giver of that which you have received.

There is a story in Luke 5 about a man who was paralyzed. His friends heard that Jesus was going to be nearby and had heard of the miracles that had happened in His presence. So in faith, wanting their friend to be healed, they planned to take their friend to Jesus. So they put their friend on a mat of sorts. I envision it having some type of cord or rope on each of the four corners because scripture says that they carried him.

When they got to the house where Jesus was inside teaching, there was such a crowd gathered, there was no way to push through. In desperation, and because I'm sure they had come this far and didn't want to turn back now, they devised a plan to hoist their friend up to the roof, which they did. Then the paralytic's friends started tearing away the thatching from the roof to create a hole. When the hole was big enough, the men lifted their broken brother and gently let him down through the roof of the house, bringing him to rest at the feet of Jesus. Jesus recognized the faith of this broken man's friends.

It is there that I wish to pick up in Luke 5:

When Jesus saw their faith, he said, "Friend, your sins are forgiven." The Pharisees and the teachers of the law began thinking to themselves, "Who is this fellow who

speaks blasphemy? Who can forgive sins but God alone?" Jesus knew what they were thinking and asked, "Why are you thinking these things in your hearts? Which is easier: to say, 'Your sins are forgiven,' or to say, 'Get up and walk'? But I want you to know that the Son of Man has authority on earth to forgive sins." So he said to the paralyzed man, "I tell you, get up, take your mat and go home." Immediately he stood up in front of them, took what he had been lying on and went home praising God. Everyone was amazed and gave praise to God. They were filled with awe and said, "We have seen remarkable things today." (vs. 20-26 NIV)

I want to point out something to you in this story that may help better illustrate what has happened with you and me. Jesus' first response wasn't to heal this man of his physical brokenness. Christ knew that even though the young men, in faith, had brought their friend to Him for healing, Jesus knew that the *primary* need was that of an eternal nature. So Jesus forgave his sin, not out of a *lack* of compassion, but out of the very *height* of it.

Notice the grumbling of the Pharisees that followed. They considered what Jesus had done to be blasphemy, saying in their hearts, "Who can forgive sins but God alone?" Jesus had performed a miracle, but these people could not see it with their own eyes. Their *spiritual* sight had been constrained by the limits of their *physical* sight.

Friends, *we* have been in the same place as that paralyzed man. Now I didn't have four friends to take me to Jesus as he did. Heck, I looked around and could barely scrape up *one* that was within reach. But just as that young man did, I found myself at the feet of Jesus paralyzed by my sin, my past, my shame, my regret, my fear...you get the picture. You've been there, too.

On that floor in the altar of Gateway Church in Texas, God met me and forgave my sin. My other needs went lacking at the time, not out of a *lack* of compassion, but out of the very *height* of it. As I've told others about my encounters with Jesus and the forgiveness and grace I've received; they've grumbled just as the Pharisees did in Jesus' day. They've reminded me that to them I'm still paralyzed. They tell me that I've made my own bed and I have to lay in it; that I am defined by the "bed" (my sin) carrying me.

Scripture says that Jesus knew what they were saying in their hearts, called them on it. Jesus' response to their blindness to the work of God that was taking place before them was to give them something they could see with their physical eyes. In doing so, He pointed out that their spiritual eyes were being constrained by the limits of the physical. There was neither faith nor a discerning spirit that existed among them, yet they were the religious leaders of the day. So Jesus gave them something they *could* see with their physical eyes so they would know "that the Son of Man has authority on earth to forgive sins."

Many may miss what I'm about to point out to you. I missed it myself the first thousand times I read or heard this account. But in Jesus' directive to the paralyzed man, he didn't just tell him to "get up and go home." Jesus told him to "get up, *take up your mat* and go home." (Emphasis mine)

Did you get that? I almost want to shout, friends! There was grumbling about Jesus telling this man that his sins were forgiven, right? We've heard grumbling too, haven't we? We've seen our friends turn and walk away. We've heard how we don't deserve grace, but we already *knew* that. We found that out just by reading the definition of grace. God just gave it to us anyway. But here's the point that I want you to remember about our paralytic friend. Jesus could have just told him to get up and go home. That would have surely been enough for these naysayers to see that Jesus' words carried power behind them. But Jesus included the part about taking up his mat too. *That young man took hold of that which once had taken hold of him. And he walked!* That which defined him was now defined *by* him. He suddenly had a new worldview, and by God's grace, so do we. We no longer see things from lying flat on our backs, down for the count. We can *STAND!* And our perspective on life looks a lot different when we're upright and walking.

Lessons learned while getting up:

1. God Adores You.

2. Grace: Can't Qualify. Can't Disqualify.

3. There's Strength In the Journey.

4. The Difference Between Content and Enough

5. Who I Say, I Am

6. Forgiving Is Essential

7. The Mind Is the Door to Your Life

8. A Changed Life Brings A Changed Perspective

What lessons did God teach you as you read this chapter?

Today's Date: _____

_____

_____

_____

_____

_____

_____

_____

_____

_____

_____

_____

_____

_____

_____

_____

_____

_____

_____

_____

_____

_____

_____

_____

_____

Chapter 9
There Is Assured Hope

A New Beginning

Our perspective has changed quite drastically since first we met. We started chapter one on the floor. We ended the last chapter standing and having taken hold of that which once had taken hold of us. No longer defined by our past, but by the word of God, we face today's challenges with a new outlook. That stirring in our bellies is no longer from *anxiety*, but from *anticipation*. Like our former paralytic friend from the last chapter, we are free to be excited about what the day will bring and what God will do in and through us, as we pursue our passions to fulfill our purposes and claim His promises to us.

Friends, don't worry about what people will say about you. They may say that the grace you claim isn't valid. They may deny that God is doing amazing things in your life, all for which you give Him the credit. That's okay. How do you think our Pharisee characters responded to that young man standing up and walking out? Scripture doesn't really say. They may have claimed it to be some form of illusion or magic. But their claims didn't change the miracle to the paralytic. Whatever they may have said about him didn't change the fact that he was walking home with a mat under his arm. Their words would not have affected the story that he was going to tell to anyone who had ears to hear in the coming days. His stories would only be filled with the words of Jesus, not the words of others who tried to dumb down the power of the very Son of God. He was a man with an experience. The Pharisees merely had an argument.

As I write this, the sun has just come up here in Nashville, and its beams are bursting through my sliding glass door. I'm reminded of Lamentations 3:22-23 (NLT) that says, "The faithful love of the lord never ends! His mercies never cease. Great is his faithfulness; his mercies begin afresh each morning." The forgiveness of God isn't "one and done." *Every morning* He is waiting for us to get up so He can greet us with the new day He made. And every sunrise brings new mercies from our Heavenly Father.

Can you imagine what it must have been like for the young, formerly paralyzed man when he first woke up the next morning? I wonder if by habit he reached for a bell to ring for help to move about for his morning routine before he remembered...*I can walk!* It wasn't just the fact that he could walk; *everything* became new. What had been his *normal* was now all different. *Good,* but different.

There would be no more sliding across the floor and scuffing knees and elbows, as he would drag himself from one point to the next in his home. All of the bells he used to ring for help probably went into a yard sale. He could go to market by himself, ride a camel, and maybe even have the family he'd only dreamed of having before.

That's another word that has changed somewhat in perspective for us, hasn't it? *Before*. Early on, we used *before* to describe the time prior to our mistakes. It was the time period when life was enjoyed, and the flames had not started feeding on us and changing us. *Before* we were grossly disfigured by our past.

Now *before* tells of a time of despair and turmoil because we're in a *new* place. *Before* carries in its bowels the story of a broken individual who was lost, desperate, and dying. Sadness surrounds its tales of worry, anxiety, depression, and suicidal thoughts. Now, all of that was *before*. It was before we let light into our lives and let truth reveal what filled our hidden dark corners. Before we had passion, purpose, and promise. Before we knew what should really be considered home for us. Before Jesus. Before grace. Before hope.

Who we were *before,* what we did *before,* where we were *before,* doesn't matter. I used to speak of who I was *before* thinking that it was only in proper context if used meaning "prior to deciding to follow Jesus." *Before,* when used in conversation, would have the same meaning as B.C. when speaking of years in history. It was my *before Christ* time.

Now, *before* sometimes means *yesterday,* or even *five minutes ago.* I need the mercy, forgiveness, and grace of God *daily.* I'm so glad that He gave us Lamentations 3:22-23. His mercy is new every day, which is exactly how I need it. He knew my life would be filled with many *before's* and that I would need Him for every single one of them. Yes, He knew I needed that. My guess is you do, too.

This mercy, this grace, cost Jesus His very *life.* To use such a thing as a license to sin, and giving the old "easier to ask forgiveness than permission" type excuse doesn't fly with God. To do that makes a mockery out of what cost Him so much. Romans 6:1-2 (NLT) instructs us, "Well then, should we keep on sinning so that God can show us more and more of his wonderful grace? Of course not! Since we have died to sin, how can we continue to live in it?" But my guess is that, if you're like me, the closer you've gotten to Jesus and have had the light of His holiness illumine your heart, the more correctly you have seen even the smallest of your sin. When this happens, one looks at grace differently. You think of grace as such a precious treasure that you would never even *want* to use it for such an excuse. Show me a person who still believes that people use Biblical grace as an excuse for sin, and I will show you a person who still does not have a correct view of their sin in light of holiness.

There is one thing from *before* that still is, however. And that is your calling on your life - your purpose. Just as His love cannot be taken away from you, God tells us in Romans 11:29 (NIV), "God's gifts and his call are irrevocable." Our past never robbed us of our purpose. No matter what mess we've made of our lives, God has very unique ways of turning our *mess* into our *ministry*.

Through

"The best way out is always through."   - Robert Frost

Notice that Frost didn't say the *easiest* way out was through; he said the *best* way. *Through* is rarely easy in real life. Ask anyone who has been *through* a health crisis, financial crisis, emotional crisis, the death of loved ones, the addictions of children, any war you can name, they will all tell you that *through* was tough. Resistance resides around every corner.

I said it earlier, and I'll say it again, testimonies are only formed through testing. Have you ever been in a setting where you felt encouraged and inspired because someone told their life story and, come to find out, they had never had one rough spot their entire lives? No! Of course, not. The stories we want to hear more than *any* other are those stories where someone has been through something *hard*, and we see that they made it. People want to know that there is hope.

Are you a fan of some of the singing talent shows on TV? I am. As a musician, I am a little picky about which ones I watch. If you've seen any of these shows over time, you've undoubtedly seen a young teenager try singing a song about being hurt by love, or some other subject matter that is obviously outside their ability to have experienced at their current age. To those of us who are listening, the believability of the performance lessens. We may like the song and enjoy the beat, but in our minds we're thinking, "but this *kid* has never experienced what they're singing about." The believability lessens considerably in those situations.

When people are sitting in church and they hear sermons or testimonies by others, there are times when the same reactions take place. They know whether or not the person speaking has ever really been in the trenches of life to experience that about which they speak. People do it all the time, though, don't they? They try to act like an authority on a subject and pretend they know enough about another's circumstance to speak some kind of truth into their lives. But they're not believable. The lack of experience betrays their efforts every time. People know when you're trying to fool them. They can hear the hurt in the voice and see the pain in the eyes. They know.

This is the reason that I wrote this book. As I looked back at my life and the mistakes I've made, and as I revisit the times in my mind of being on the floor, I know I'm not the only one who has been there. Someone out there, maybe you, is seeing what I've been through and is identifying with me. I'm not the first, and I certainly won't be the last. There have been multiple points in my life where I wish I could've picked up a book or heard someone with experience speak about hope.

Though I didn't want this book to be an exposé, I knew that I would have to include enough of the story of my sin that you and others reading this would know that I've been where you are. There are many who would disagree with me, but I would encourage you as you move forward to be open with where you've been. There needs to be a level of responsibility with that; it's true. But when we just generalize our struggles and just throw it all under the "sin" umbrella, we miss the opportunity for others to see the hope in us to its highest level.

I've been that guy sitting in the pew on a Sunday hearing someone tell their story of hope. The speaker never mentioned what their personal struggle included. So I sat there and said to myself, "Even though I can tell they've been through *something*, it couldn't have been as serious as what I've been through. There's no hope for me like that. I could *never* tell anyone about my story." Have you ever thought that? I remember the first time I went to a Promise Keepers rally, the Christian men's group that was popular back in the 90's, and I heard other men speak truthfully about certain sins that had been included in their struggles, and I remember thinking how freeing the experience was for me because I knew then that I wasn't alone. There was *power* in those rallies because we were *real* with each other. Even though Christ had intended that for the Church, somewhere along the way, we dropped that kind of reality with each other. We'll speak more about this in Appendix A.

I've also come to understand that the testing that I go *through* isn't just to give us a story to tell. God has given us an assurance in scripture. The Bible tells us, "So be strong and courageous! Do not be afraid and do not panic before them. For the lord your God will personally go ahead of you. He will neither fail you nor abandon you." (Deuteronomy 31:6 NLT) When times come that we know we are to go *through*, we have the peace of knowing that God, Himself, goes before us. He does this to act as a shield for us. Before we take the first step to our *through*, God sees and knows exactly how He will bring us *out*. Since we cannot give what we do not first possess, we need to *know* that we have the hope we claim before we *give* testimony to others. This is why there must be a *through* to our journey.

We can rest a moment now and realize that we do indeed have hope. That our hope is a *confident* hope. It is not a wish, but something you can literally stake your life upon. But don't get too comfortable. The enemy isn't through with us. He will keep coming in the ways we've outlined. We can bank on that for the rest of our lives. Just remember, however, that which you have learned here. This hope is *always* available. God is never further from us than a whisper of His name.

You will need to know that there is hope again one day. Keep this book handy. Remember what we've discussed and what you have written down at the end of each chapter as God has made even more revelations to you in personal ways. Though the methods will be the same, the next time the adversary attacks; things will look a little different. He knows you learned a lesson this time, but he won't stop. You are too strong in your purpose now for him to simply leave you alone. You now carry a testimony of hope. You have been tested. And you have come *through*.

Therefore, we will need to be better prepared next time. Our faith must be strengthened along with our resolve. God knows that, and He knows ahead of time the tools that we will need to handle what the adversary will end up using against us. Our Heavenly Father has promised us that we will never face a temptation that He won't make a way out for us (1 Corinthians 10:13). So just know that there will be trials to come. God hasn't forgotten you or turned His back on you as friends have done before, He's only strengthening you, knowing what the enemy will use against you. There is a way out. There is hope.

One of my favorite passages of scripture is taken from Isaiah 43. It says: "But now, O Jacob, listen to the lord who created you. O Israel, the one who formed you says, 'Do not be afraid, for I have ransomed you. I have called you by name; you are mine. When you go through deep waters, I will be with you. When you go through rivers of difficulty, you will not drown. When you walk through the fire of oppression, you will not be burned up; the flames will not consume you. For I am the lord, your God, the Holy One of Israel, your Savior.'" (vs. 1-3a NLT)

These verses let us know that going through a testing is not an *if*, it's a *when*. Note what the scripture says again: "*When* you pass through the waters," "*when* you pass through the rivers," "*when* you walk through the fire." There will be times in your life when you will feel overwhelmed. You will feel like the fire may consume you or like you will drown in the deep water. The fire and the water are necessary for testing.

Remember, God isn't allowing these things to test *us* so much; He's allowing these things to happen so that He can show us that *He* stands the test. Remember that He has called you by His name for you that defines your purpose. If we go through deep water and fire *alone*, we're going to drown. We're going to get burned! That's the nature of those elements, and there's no way to stop it. They consume. God designed them that way. God isn't granting us magical powers of some sort either. He's saying that He will be there with us, and He will *protect* us. The fire and water is a chance for God to prove Himself to us that He is as good as His word.

In the promise of His protection, this passage also gives us the way we will need to go in each case: "When you pass *through* the waters," "when you pass *through* the rivers," "when you walk *through* the fire." Scripture says much more about what we go *through* or find ourselves in, than what we go around. And even then, most of the time, an *around* journey often involves wandering, indecision, and disobedience. God's not into wasting our time or His. The shortest distance between two points is still a straight line. And, for us, that means...*through.*

So, yes, hard times will certainly come. Uncertainty will mark days and even seasons of our lives. We will seek God's face. We will dream of easier times when moments of rest will fuel our toil more efficiently. We will question God. And questioning God is fine with Him as long as His answer is fine with you and not a condition of your obedience. You may even find that the answer you seek is in the question you ask. Life teaches us that there are indeed many times when questions tell us more than answers.

Nothing *great* ever happens in safety. It is only when He is our *only* hope that we come to trust in the hope we have in Him. It is indeed a confident hope. If we want all God has for us, we must go out into the deep. We can't receive His full measure staying in shallow water where our feet can touch the bottom and *we* are the ones in control. Trust can't be learned that way.

Just as certain as the water and fire, so is *through*. The water and fire are not destinations; they are but passing moments. What awaits us on the other side is renewed hope. God's ways and thoughts for us are so much higher than our own for ourselves. He has promised that even in times of trouble, He will never leave nor forsake us. He walks before us. He holds our hand. And soon, hope will come yet again. Past hope will be strengthened. New hope will be born. Romans 5:3-4 (NIV): "Not only so, but we also glory in our sufferings, because we know that suffering produces perseverance; perseverance, character; and character, hope." But first we must go *through*.

Focus

The object of our attention determines our direction. If you're a NASCAR fan, or have ever heard drivers talk about things they are taught when learning to drive, you may have heard that it is *drilled* into them to *never* look at the wall. Why? Because they know that if they look at the wall, they will drive right into it. They are taught to focus on where they want the car to go instead. Instructors know that where the eyes go, the wheels are soon to follow.

As we move forward in hope, join me in doing so with a focus on Jesus Christ. He's our shield, our protector, our fortress. He stands guard at the door to our lives - our minds. His word is active and alive in us and we are co-heirs with Him to all God has given Him. If He is for us, who can be against us? Why would you ever want to focus on anything or anyone *else?*

As it says in Hebrews 12:1-2 (NIV), "Therefore, since we are surrounded by such a great cloud of witnesses, let us throw off everything that hinders and the sin that so easily entangles. And let us run with perseverance the race marked out for us, fixing our eyes on Jesus, the pioneer and perfecter of faith. For the joy set before him he endured the cross, scorning its shame, and sat down at the right hand of the throne of God."

There is an entire world out there full of people who are just like you and me and going through the same waters and fires. The names and locations may be different, but the pain is the same. They have a past. They have fears. They're on the floor and they're begging for hope. *Yours* is a story that needs to be told. No matter how insignificant you believe it to be, there is always someone that needs *your* story. There's something special and unique about your story that may make the difference between life and death for someone else. It may even be your relationship to them that makes the difference that someone else's story, or even this book, could never make.

Just as Malachi 3 talks about robbing God of tithes and offerings, I believe with all my heart that when we don't share our stories of hope to a world *without* hope, that we are *robbing God* of the glory He rightly deserves. And we also break His heart knowing that if His heart beats for others, and we deny them the hope we have come to know, we are withholding that blessing of God on our lives as well.

Friends, Jesus didn't offer the world a strategy for moral behavior; He offered to reconnect them to life. He didn't die to make bad people good, He died to make dead people alive. This is our hope! This is what we claim as our promise. Right now, we have the assured hope of eternal life. But a day will soon come when our hope will be our reality. Every promise will be fulfilled. Our faith will be made sight. We will hear a name called for the very first time - the name that God the Father has for us that only we can understand.

Until then, we stand, no longer laid out on the floor. We got up. We took hold of that which once took hold of us and we press on knowing that our perseverance will build our character, and our character builds our hope each day. In relationship with Jesus, hope is more noun than verb, more expectation than method, more fact than wish. It's an assured promise. Live in it!

Lessons learned while getting up:

1. God Adores You.

2. Grace: Can't Qualify. Can't Disqualify.

3. There's Strength In the Journey.

4. The Difference Between Content and Enough

5. Who I Say, I Am

6. Forgiving Is Essential

7. The Mind Is the Door to Your Life

8. A Changed Life Brings A Changed Perspective

9. There Is Assured Hope

What lessons did God teach you as you read this chapter?

Today's Date: _____

_____
_____
_____
_____
_____
_____
_____
_____
_____
_____
_____
_____
_____
_____
_____
_____
_____
_____
_____
_____
_____
_____
_____
_____
_____
_____

Appendix A
How Should A Church Handle the Moral Failure of A Staff Member?

As a result of not only my personal failures, but also having witnessed first-hand churches handling these situations, this is a question I get asked with some frequency. I will say this; it's *never* easy. Frankly, you may not like my answer, and that's okay. You have that right. But since the question has been posed to me numerous times, I've chosen to answer it here.

Before any action whatsoever is taken, you must first realize that what you are dealing with is spiritual warfare. It's not to be taken lightly. The enemy is out to get our churches. Scripture plainly says, as we've already discussed, that the gates of hell won't even prevail against the Church. But one person, someone in leadership, is a prime target for him. The moment *any* person enters the ministry, there is an immediate target placed on their back by the enemy. It's like taking down the field commanding officer in battle. The army becomes less effective with no direct command on the field.

Also know that how you treat the situation will be planting the seed for how *you* will possibly be treated at some point in the future. We *all* think we will never do anything of the sort. We all claim to be more in control of our emotions, too in love with our spouses, too focused because of children, too mature to ever be involved in some type of moral sin. Just because one is not prone to addiction, doesn't mean that he or she won't be addicted to something in their lifetime. My wife, who is an incredibly Godly woman and not prone to addiction, will tell you that one of the hardest things she has ever done was coming off narcotic pain killers following surgery back in 2005. There are ways the enemy can get us all.

What you need to realize going into this is that God is not the only one watching how you handle yourself. The enemy is, too. He's got his eye on the Church. If she doesn't respond according to scripture, if *you* don't respond Biblically, he will bank that information and it may be used against you at some point in the future.

Time after time I was told that my friends leaving me, and the way that others were treating me, was my just due; that I was "reaping what I had sown." I'm sure I was. I don't deny that fact. But so will you. If you treat a brother or sister in that manner and fail to show

Godly grace, *when* that time comes in your life (notice I said *when* not *if*), you can expect that there will be a great chance you will be treated likewise. To withhold grace from someone in need of it is just as grave a sin as the one committed by the one in need of grace. Whatever seeds you sow here with your brother or sister *will* grow and be ready for harvest one day. It may be you, a sibling, a child, a parent, someone. But there will be a need for grace. Count on it. And remember these words you read when it comes. You will one day seek from others that which is being sought from you. Act carefully and wisely. If you're in church leadership, that same target is on your back too.

Prevention

The best way to deal with this situation is for it to never happen to begin with. I think we all could agree with that. Yet we are seeing staggering numbers of fallen staff members across America today. This raises the question, why?

Many churches don't start with **accountability** to their staff, especially the pastor. Now understand, I'm *not* saying *at all* that churches should have a system where the pastor can't make decisions without having to run everything through a board of deacons or elders! Deacons and elders are great to have. But Biblically, their roles are strictly service oriented and have nothing to do with the day-to-day operations or decisions of the church. The pastor is the under-shepherd of the church and is charged with setting the vision and providing leadership in the general direction of the church. They are to feed the sheep and protect the pulpit by screening others who feed their sheep.

My point is that every leader needs some people he can trust to use as sounding boards for major decisions for the church. These can be deacons or elders, but they can also be laymen or laywomen within the church.

Let's be honest, church folk can be downright mean and ornery sometimes. Leaders never want to make decisions under certain circumstances without running those decisions through some trusted advisors first. The circumstances in which one doesn't need to make a decision are easily remembered by thinking of the word: *HALT!* Don't make big decisions if you are:

- **H**urt

- **A**ngry

- **L**onely

- **T**ired

Not only is it unwise to make decisions on behalf of the church when feeling one or more of these things, it's just as unwise to make personal decisions as well. People turn to others with whom they have no business relying on when operating from these four emotions. Danger always looms ahead. Because of this, *personal accountability* should also be encouraged.

Notice that I said, "encouraged," not "mandated." When dealing with the personal life of a staff member, I don't believe it to be the role of the church to start dictating much in regard to one's personal life. The personal definitely has influence on the professional, but the church has to respect a certain amount of privacy in regard to this staff member's family. However, certain guidelines in regard to protecting the person's character in the community are to be expected.

The point is that the staff member has someone to whom he or she is accountable on a personal level and that this person's identity is made available to a body/committee/team within the church. I'm not of the opinion that the accountability partner needs to be sanctioned or approved by the church or anybody therein, just that the identity is made known upon request.

It's also wise to **protect computers in the church**. With pornography being so easily accessible to anyone with a computer, the church needs to protect their staff from temptation during the *after*-hours time spent in the offices. Software is available these days that will either prevent someone from accessing these types of web sites, or alert an assigned accountability person if access is attempted. The latter is best, in my experience, as the former blocks too many legitimate sites and becomes quite frustrating.

Next in the area of prevention is **protecting the staff member's time with their families.** As Pastors over various groups within the church, or as Senior Pastors, we know the drill when we sign on. We know that we are technically on call 24/7 whenever we're needed. But many times church members call for minute issues that are really too small to worry about, or could be handled at another more opportune time.

At the same time, many churches have experienced the staff member who is the workaholic. This type of behavior won't earn any kind of heavenly merit badge and is damaging not only to the staff member's relationship to his or her family, but can also lead to certain types of physical health issues as well.

And lastly, one of the best ways to prevent bad things from happening is to **love and pray for your staff daily**. Their entire lives are devoted to the people within the walls of your church. They need to know that they have your support and that you care about them. Let them know on a regular basis and share with them *specifically* how you pray for them.

Going back to First Christian Church in Decatur, IL, my lead guitar player, Mark, was the best prayer partner I've ever had. I counted on him the entire time I was there to be praying for me. To my knowledge, he never let me down even *once*. Not only would he pray, but he sent me emails during the day or before trips while I'd be waiting at the airport basically giving me bullet points of how he was praying for me that day. There have been times I've called Mark since leaving just because I trust him and know that this Godly man knows how to bend the ear of God!

Recap of Preventative Measures:

1. Professional and Personal Accountability

2. Church Computer Protection

3. Church Protecting Family Time for Staff

4. Church Loving and Praying for Staff

Start with Truth

In the unfortunate circumstance that preventative measures don't work and a failure takes place, *truth* is step one. The first truth that the church leadership and the church membership needs fully understand is that *their sin is no worse than anything you have ever done.* Theologically, all sin is equal in the way that each of them separately or collectively would have still cost Jesus His life. Sociologically, we may have put more weight on some than others. But *holiness* looks at it from a different angle.

Holiness is that for which we strive, not righteousness. We are no less righteous at the depth of our sin than we are at the height of our obedience. That's because our righteousness is not *ours* at all. Our *only* righteousness comes from a relationship with Jesus. So in your treatment of the fallen staff member, remember that they are no less righteous than you. Maybe a little less holy, but no less righteous.

I don't care what the circumstance, whether in one's personal life, or dealing with the business life of a church staff member, you *always* start with truth. I've seen churches try to protect both parties where there has been an affair or try to soften the language when there has been a porn addiction. This has proven to be unwise in every case I've experienced.

Rumor is always worse than truth. And there's nothing like a good scandal to bring out the gossipers and witch hunters from every nook and cranny of the community! If you use phrases like "moral failure" or "moral misjudgment" (both of which I've heard used), you open the doors wide open for speculation.

The most recent event that I have seen to use as an example is with Pastor Jim (again, not his real name) from Chapter 6. SouthWay Church (not the real name either) had no real system of accountability. Pastor Jim made decisions right and left however he wanted to do things. As I pointed out, things ran amuck from staff turnover, to budgeting, to relationships with staff and church members, to his lack of leadership ability.

It cost him and the church dearly. Jim recently resigned SouthWay. The reason given was "several instances of moral misjudgment." You should have seen the feeding frenzy that happened online as a result. Over 1,000 posts from church members, people in the community, all drawing their own conclusions of what "moral misjudgment" could mean.

Then it appeared on the county web site that his wife had filed for divorce. And do you know what was called into question mostly? It wasn't Pastor Jim's failures. It was the lack of accountability for him by the church. This whole mess could have been avoided had the proper accountability been in place.

Though I understand the thought process behind it, the determination was made that Jim not appear before the congregation. There can be advantages and disadvantages to this, and each case would need to be prayerfully weighed out to see which course of action would be necessary.

If the staff member in question has anger toward the church or individuals in the church that may cause him or her to exhibit an out of order outburst in front of the collective church, then the staff member most definitely should *not* appear before the collective church. But truth should *still* be the foundation! It just may need to come from someone other than the staff member in that situation.

On the flip side, if the staff member in question seems to be truly sorry for what they did and is submitting to the leadership of the church, then, in my opinion and according to James 5:13-16, the staff member should confess their sin openly to the church.

I know several of you just swallowed your biscuits whole. But seriously, let's quit having a double standard as a church. If a husband steps out on his wife, we would, of course, expect that man to come clean with his bride. It was not only against God that he sinned, but against her as well.

The same is true here within the church. The staff member in question would have not only sinned against God, but the church as well. Though this sin may have been private, the sin was against the church as this staff member is a paid leader within the church.

Let's see here what James 5 has to say:

"Are any of you suffering hardships? You should pray. Are any of you happy? You should sing praises. Are any of you sick? You should call for the elders of the church to come and pray over you, anointing you with oil in the name of the Lord. Such a prayer offered in faith will heal the sick, and the Lord will make you well. And if you have committed any sins, you will be forgiven. Confess your sins to each other and pray for each other so that you may be healed. The earnest prayer of a righteous person has great power and produces wonderful results." (vs. 13-16 NLT)

1 Timothy 5:19-21 (NLT) is a little more pointed when talking about handling an elder (staff member): "Do not listen to an accusation against an elder unless it is confirmed by two or three witnesses. Those who sin *should be reprimanded in front of the whole church*; this will serve as a strong warning to others. I solemnly command you in the presence of God and Christ Jesus and the highest angels to obey these instructions *without taking sides or showing favoritism to anyone.*" (Emphasis mine)

We have given the enemy permission to invade our churches by our unwillingness to stick to scripture. We no longer confess our sins to one another. As a matter of fact, the Church has made it taboo in the name of keeping others from being embarrassed. That is a weapon of the enemy. What if the natural ethos of the church *was* confessing our sins to each other? What if that was normal practice every week in our services? What would happen?

1. There would be no need to be embarrassed because we would know that everyone has the same struggles we do on personal levels. We could understand each other more.

2. The church would learn the true art of forgiveness and restoration with the extension of

209

grace as our Heavenly Father meant it. There would be no turning out and kicking of our brothers and sisters, but rather a holding out of helping hands to pick them up again.

3.   There could be a time of learning in every situation where we would learn more about the heart of God for our lives by watching how He responds in the lives of those around us.

But the enemy has *deceived* us in the past and made us believe at one point that this was not the best way to do things. And now, we've waited so long that it is harder than ever to return to the way that God prescribed for His Church.

I have been a part of this tearing away from scripture and never realized it. It wasn't the *sin du jour* that we staff members had our eyes on, but I believe what we have done is that we have indeed sinned as a Church collective. We have gone against the word of God and claimed to have a better way so as not to cause any shame or embarrassment. Yet if we'd only done it God's way there wouldn't have *been* shame and embarrassment to begin with.

Destination Restoration

I'm sorry. I don't believe that 12 Step programs and predetermined therapy sessions with counselors who take people through a curriculum are always the best way. Notice I used the word *always*. There are times when these programs can indeed affect needed change in a person's behavior and life. They can give you some warning signs that will give you directions along your journey. My point is, counseling programs only give you the tools to use, but it's still up to *you* to use them.

I know that if my best friend were out there reading this, he would strongly disagree with me here. His whole point of severing the relationship was that he felt I needed intense counseling and around-the-clock accountability while living in some form of an institution. *Maybe* that would've helped, but money wouldn't allow it at the time he demanded it. I believe God had a better plan, however. And to be honest, I think it was even harder than what I would've experienced in a predetermined program that was designed by man.

In the main section of the book, I referenced Matthew 18, which is commonly referred to as the "church discipline chapter." It's really not. It is a step-by-step manual on restoration. Here, read it for yourself:

"If another believer sins against you, go privately and point out the offense. If the other person listens and confesses it, you have won that person back. But if you are unsuccessful, take one or two others with you and go back again, so that two or three witnesses may confirm everything you say. If the person still refuses to listen, take your case to the church. Then if he or she won't accept the church's decision, treat that person as a pagan or a corrupt tax collector. I tell you the truth, whatever you forbid on earth will be forbidden in heaven, and whatever you permit on earth will be permitted in heaven. I also tell you this: If two of you agree here on earth concerning anything you ask, my Father in heaven will do it for you. For where two or three gather together as my followers, I am there among them." (vs. 15-20 NLT)

There are three steps that are outlined here prior to any turning away. Turning them away has become our first go-to action, has it not? We tend to put the offender out to pasture and just pretend it didn't happen within ourselves and circle the wagons so that the rotten apple doesn't spoil the whole bunch. We then carry on as usual, ignoring the cries of help from outside the wagon circle, because we've been afraid of the consequences in the offering plates. We go on with planned sermon series and sweep it all under the ministry rugs as quickly as possible. If a guest walks in the next week, our goal is that they never know anything has happened. We want them to feel secure and that they are walking in to a group of *good* people. Can anyone besides me see the problem here? We need more leaders with the backbone to *lead through* these circumstances, not avoid them.

Look at the instruction given to the church in Galatians 6:

"Dear brothers and sisters, if another believer is overcome by some sin, you who are godly should gently and humbly help that person back onto the right path. And be careful not to fall into the same temptation yourself. Share each other's burdens, and in this way obey the law of Christ. If you think you are too important to help someone, you are only fooling yourself. You are not that important." (vs. 1-3 NLT)

As I discussed in the main portion of the book, we Christians have a *strong desire* to keep our hands clean. Every action we take is viewed first from that frame of reference. So we've looked at this verse, completely ignoring the section saying to restore a fellow believer who has been overcome by sin, and jumped right to the "be careful not to fall into the same temptation yourself" part. We can stay clean that way *and* keep it "scriptural." If asked if we tried to restore, we just reply, "Naw. Too Dangerous. Why, I might've fallen into that temptation myself." Can I just throw the bovine scatology flag right there?

James 5:19-20 talks about the potential of what could happen from our obedience. "My dear brothers and sisters, if someone among you wanders away from the truth and is brought back, you can be sure that whoever brings the sinner back from wandering will save that person from death and bring about the forgiveness of many sins." (NLT)

Lastly, a passage that comes from 1 Peter 5:10, "In his kindness God called you to share in his eternal glory by means of Christ Jesus. So after you have suffered a little while, he will restore, support, and strengthen you, and he will place you on a firm foundation." (NLT)

Church, that is *NOT* your directive toward the person in question to make them "suffer a little while." Scripture never says to turn your back on a brother or sister without first getting your hands dirty and doing everything in your power to bring them back and restore them.

It is not your duty to dish out consequences, no matter how you feel. They may have hurt you. They may have lied to you. They may have sinned against the God you both serve. But "there is no condemnation" from God, and there shouldn't be from you either.

Every action must be predicated on love. Let's look at scripture again. "So now I am giving you a new commandment: Love each other. Just as I have loved you, you should love each other. Your love for one another will prove to the world that you are my disciples." (John 13:34-35 NLT) Growing up, I sang a song in church that said, "Yes, they'll know we are Christians by our love." That line is only half right. According to Jesus, as the John 13 verses are in red letters being the words of Christ, Himself, the way the world will know we are Christians is by our love...for each other.

That's not how we've done it, though, is it? Intentions have been right. But our standard protocol when we see Christians getting caught in public committing some sort of sin, normally looks very little like what Jesus prescribed. Instead there is something a little closer to this scenario: Cameras roll, headlines print, police lights flash, Twitter feeds trend, and news anchors report. Suddenly we feel that the name of God is getting bad press. So we steal a page from the weekly SURVIVOR television script. We cast our votes to evict, call the offenders to the front, tell them "the tribe has spoken," put out their torch, and send them packing. Embarrassment over. Problem solved. Crisis averted. We've saved the reputation of the Church in the view of those outside the Church. Or so we think.

But what about the love issue from John 13? We are to love them as Christ has loved us. Is an eviction what He would have done? Where is the forgiveness, grace, and mercy in that action? Scripture tells us the gates of hell itself will not prevail against the Church. So, in light of that Biblical proclamation, what does some guy named Tom, or Steve, or whoever, who is struggling with a porn problem or a drug addiction, have to bring against the Church that the gates of hell itself cannot? Why would we think that a human being could cause much more damage to the Kingdom that the forces of hell? It makes no sense when you think about it, does it?

People, who are not affiliated with Christ or any church, look at Christians and call us hypocrites. We've gotten it into our heads that the reason they do this is because of exposed sin. No! People outside our walls aren't stupid. They know we sin. They may not label it as such, but they know sin is a part of the human condition.

No matter what kind of best foot we try to put forward, all feet carry a little "stank" with them. They're feet. That's their curse in life. Try as you might, neither you nor anyone else will be able to make the world think you have your act completely, maybe not even mostly, together. The world outside the Church knows we sin. They see it. They're in the secret places we go to try and hide our vices. They see our attitudes and senses of entitlement in restaurants and retail stores. (Having worked in retail, ask any retail worker, they will tell you that Christians have the worst reputations of all customers as being rude, tipping small, and having senses of entitlement coupled with perceived superiority.) They know we are not altogether as good and important as we think we are. Many are even laughing at us behind our backs because we have ourselves so fooled.

Then when the light shines on one of us for what the world already knows we have done, we speak as a "tribe," evict our own, and try to say it was an isolated incident. We say that we would have never let them into our "tribe" if we had known they were capable of such things. Such people become completely blackballed and exiled away from the bunch. (Let me take a moment to remind you of the 99 and 1 and how our adversary waits on one to be separated or injured to devour them.)

Friends, the world doesn't think us hypocrites because we sin. They think us hypocrites because we try to hide our sin and/or pretend we don't sin. They're wondering what has happened to the forgiveness that we claim to extend to others. They have no interest in Jesus because of our actions. They think, with good reason, that if we would do that to one of our own, why wouldn't we do likewise to them? It's like we offer grace until someone signs on the dotted line and becomes a member, then grace takes a back seat to our reputation as a church.

Jesus said that the world will know us by our love for each other. Caring isn't good enough. Love is the standard. A desire to protect the Church isn't the right angle. Jesus said to love them as He has loved us. Nothing less will do. All action should be born from love.

Loving the person doesn't mean we sweep the sin under the rug. The staff member in question can expect some type of pain. Sin causes that. There needs to be an understanding that it's not God who causes the pain; it's the sin. God never reminds you of your past once the blood of Jesus is applied. Only the enemy does that. But God says that He is there with you throughout whatever fire you must walk. This pain is only for "a little while." It's not permanent. Then God's promise to you is to "restore, support, strengthen, and place you on a firm foundation."

Freedom and Healing from Sin

I've been the jailbird that was set free only to return to captivity and wonder how I ever got back in such a state. I believe that our churches are full of Christian people every Sunday who are in bondage to some sort of sin, yet feel that there is no way out. They hear about freedom, sing songs about freedom, hear testimonies about others experiencing freedom, but freedom has always seemed to elude them. Why is that? Is that what Jesus intended when He established the Church? I think not. So let's examine this for a moment.

Can we all agree that we can hide nothing from God? If you didn't know that, well...you can't. He sees all, knows all, hears all, and is over all. There's no way to get around our Heavenly Father. When we confess our sins to Him, we are simply agreeing with Him that we have done what He already knows we've done. So why is it necessary if He already knows? It's not necessary for Him. It's necessary for *us*. It's opening ourselves up to His love, holiness, forgiveness, grace, and mercy.

Scripture equates sin to darkness many times throughout. In contrast, it equates God, holiness, and righteousness to light. When light, even a small flicker, is introduced into darkness, darkness cannot hide from light. Darkness is forced to reveal its secrets.

But the revelation of secrets can be a scary thing, can't it? We don't like other people, especially someone in authority, like GOD, knowing all our junk. After all, we're programmed from the time we are kids that "good" is rewarded and "bad" is punished. We're told that Santa Claus only comes to "good" boys and girls. So we'd better watch out and we'd better not cry or pout. The first thing that's asked of a baby sitter or someone watching kids for a time by the parents on their return is, "Were they good?" When parents take their kids with them while running errands and the kids ask for candy, ice cream, toys, etc., the general answer is something like, "If you're good while we're out, I'll get you _____." And all of that is programmed into our minds during the most formative years of our lives.

So no wonder as adults, even though we may never be under authority where someone would use those words in inquiry about us, the devil has a field day with well-intended lessons we learned as children. He continues to feed the idea that we will be rewarded if we're good and punished if we're bad. So more than anything, we want to be "good" people. We don't want others to know how bad we are behind closed doors. We don't want them to find out what we watched on our computers, or the few deposits we left off our taxes, or the true intent of our hearts when we gossip in the name of a prayer request. We magnify the bad deeds of others, why? Because it makes us look "good." So why upset that apple cart?

Besides that, it's only between you and God, right? And God is the only one who can forgive sin anyway. Verses like 1 John 1:9 that says, "But if we confess our sins to him, he is faithful and just to forgive us our sins and to cleanse us from all wickedness." (NLT) That is indeed 100% correct. Only God can forgive the eternal consequence of sin through the work of Jesus on the cross. And He is faithful to do so. But what about the next time you're faced with that choice? See, sin normally isn't done in light where everybody else can see what we're doing. The things we watch on our computers, the taxes, the heart's intent; those things are all hidden from prying eyes. And the fact that they are hidden creates an environment rich in temptation.

Luke 4:19, Jesus says, "The Spirit of the Lord is on me, because he has anointed me to proclaim good news to the poor, He has sent me to proclaim freedom for the prisoners and recovery of sight for the blind, to set the oppressed free, to proclaim the year of the Lord's favor." But let's be honest. freed prisoners sometimes find their way back to captivity. (I reference the opening of this section of the book.) Before we know it, we can find ourselves back under the weight of oppression. Sin that we thought was in our past comes to surface again. Yet there is indeed freedom to be had; otherwise Jesus would be a liar. So if there is freedom, how do we experience it? Here is where God has taught me new things. Bear with me a minute, because you might not understand unless we wrap it all together and you finish with me.

There are certain parts of our salvation that are "one time only" and others that are a process. 1 Peter 3:18, Romans 6:10, Hebrews 9:27-28, Hebrews 10:12, and Hebrews 7:27, tells us that Jesus died "once" for all. His death was good enough to cover the sin of the world past, present, and future. Romans 8:35-39 reminds us that nothing in the natural or supernatural can separate us from the love of God. Our salvation is secure. But in Philippians 2:12, it tells us to "work out our salvation" and Galatians 5:4 mentions a "fall from grace." Is that contradictory? Not at all.

Everything about scripture is uniquely linked as only God could orchestrate it. However, sometimes in our reading of scripture, we tend to jump from "linked" to "equated." When we think about love, grace, mercy, and forgiveness, because it took all of them for our salvation, we tend to treat them as pretty much the same thing. They indeed are linked, but are not equal in definition nor should we treat them as such.

Love is the foundation. It started the whole relationship process. God first loved us; therefore, we can love Him. As we read earlier, nothing can separate us from His love. But love wasn't enough without the cross. Love required action for sin to be defeated, an action that Jesus even prayed could be bypassed knowing in His heart that it couldn't. Mercy won out. Jesus paid our debt. Lamentations 3:22-23 says that His mercies are "new every morning." Why do they even need to be new that much? Because we have a sin nature, and we will continue to sin post-salvation. But then there's grace. Grace is the key to salvation in Jesus. It's what His blood paid for. (Ephesians 2:8) Our faith, in who Jesus is and what He did, leads us to His grace, which is the miraculous result of the cross. It is the conduit through which flows forgiveness from the Father.

I've said it this way:

Love holds on to us.

We hold on to grace.

Mercy holds grace within reach.

I think that most of us can agree with these general truths: Confession is required for salvation. God's love for us is foundational to every aspect of our relationship with Him. Forgiveness comes through grace, which is recognized through our faith because of our belief in the work that Jesus did for us on the cross.

Then I read 2 Peter 3:18 where it says, "...you must grow in the grace and knowledge of our Lord and Savior, Jesus Christ..." Grow in grace? What does that mean? It was here that the lights started popping as God revealed things to me. The youth pastor at my church did a devotion with us as a worship team, and this verse was his text. In that devotion time I learned that there are two Greek words that translate to the English word knowledge that is used in the New Testament. One is *gnosis*. Gnosis is gaining knowledge through the study of a subject. Gnosis is what we get from school. It is what produces degrees and diplomas. The second word is *epignosis*. Epignosis is what is used in 2 Peter. Epignosis is knowledge that is gained through having an intimate relationship with someone. Peter is telling us that the growth of grace comes through getting to know Jesus more as a person through an intimate relationship with Him.

Remember when we were talking about light and dark? Holiness and sin? The desire to be good from childhood? We want to be good so badly that we view our own sin as "not being that bad." We tell "little white lies" and are quick to "just follow our hearts" even though scripture warns that the heart is "deceitfully wicked." (Jeremiah 17:9) We have gotten so busy in the pursuit of being good that we have neglected the pursuit to be holy. Holiness is what we're called to, not goodness. And they are two very different things.

Through time the devil has made us fearful of holiness because it is light, and light will illumine what we try so desperately to hide and will reveal to the world that we are not nearly as "good" as we say we are. But God says that's a GOOD thing. Here's why. When we draw close to God, His holiness shines its light into our lives and, yes, illumines the hidden places. But light kills the *power* of the hidden sin. Growing in grace *only* happens when we realize the true wretchedness of our own sin. That happens when we draw close to Christ. Our "little white lies" take on a much different and horrifying look in the pure light of holiness. Holiness from Jesus removes the veil and allows us to see our sin for what it truly is when put up against perfection. So then we need to surround ourselves with others who care and can help us "work out our salvation." Others? Yes!

Take another look at a verse we discussed earlier. James 5:13-16 says, "Are any of you suffering hardships? You should pray. Are any of you happy? You should sing praises. Are any of you sick? You should call for the elders of the church to come and pray over you, anointing you with oil in the name of the Lord. Such a prayer offered in faith will heal the sick, and the Lord will make you well. And if you have committed any sins, you will be forgiven. Confess your sins to each other and pray for each other so that you may be healed. The earnest prayer of a righteous person has great power and produces wonderful results."

Did you see that? When we ask forgiveness of God for sin, even when others pray over us and we agree, we receive forgiveness from God. But *healing* (which I believe to be primarily spiritual, but also can be the physical) comes from *confessing to each other*. There is power in Jesus, to forgive, yes, but He set up the Church, His bride, and has empowered us through His Holy Spirit. The freedom from oppression that He spoke about in Luke, freedom from sin that has seemed so elusive to the Church for so long, is found when we confess sins one to another.

Now does this mean we need to broadcast it and be reckless with how we tell it and to whom? No! But our small group is the Church. Our Christian friends are the Church. Our prayer groups, worship teams, volunteer groups, Sunday School classes, Christian golfing buddies, they're *all* the Church. The intent was to not tackle sin *alone* because...well...we can't. Our fellowship with Christ brings forgiveness, but our fellowship with each other brings healing because that's what Jesus has empowered us to bring to each other. I'm about to shout, people!

The Church has been trying to help God along, thinking that His plan wasn't complete enough or maybe even too harsh. We've wanted to protect the innocent and even protect ourselves from people who would gossip about us if they knew our hidden secrets. But when we bring the hidden to light, we negate the power that what was hidden had over us. Sin becomes *powerless* in confession just as darkness is powerless in light.

So *who* and *what* do we tell? Glad you asked. *What* would you be worried that others would find out? That's what you tell. *Who* would you be most worried about telling? That's whom you tell. Worry is a tool of the enemy, is it not? It wears on our mental state, our physical health, and can extend to our families as well. If we get the darkness into the light, we remove the cloud of worry that would otherwise hang over our heads. We invite accountability into our lives to assist in bringing freedom from the chains that held us. Our stories of hope through sin and failure become faith-building tools to the Church at large.

We talked earlier about how people sit in church pews every week and are in bondage to some kind of secret sin because they think they are alone and that their sin is worse than what others go through...because everybody else is "good." Oh, they've heard the testimonies from others who have been in "sin," but those giving their testimony didn't ever name what had held them in bondage. That leaves those in the pews thinking to himself or herself, "So surely it *must've* been just something like lying or running a stop sign. After all, they would never be guilty of something as bad as _____ like me." And they play along, all the while living in deceit trapped into feeling that they are the only ones. That is a tool of the enemy, my friends. We are to worship "in spirit and in truth." Hiding our sin, or making it appear to be better than what it was, is not truth and it does not glorify the hope we have in Jesus through His mercy, grace and forgiveness.

I know this is different from the way most Church is done today. But think what would happen if this were the norm in your church ethos. Gossip would all but disappear because it would be powerless. Compassion would increase, as those who had walked a mile would put the arms of others around their necks and support them as they travel down familiar rocky pathways. True forgiveness would be easier because we would realize we have no reason to hold a grudge. Stress would decrease due to reduced worry. Needs would be met because people could talk about their financial problems. Health would increase because sin, stress, and worry wouldn't weigh on the heart and mind. Seriously, do you see a down side? Of course not. How many of you would like to be a part of a church with those kinds of freedoms and a total lack of judgment from peers? I believe with all my heart that this is what Jesus had in mind when He instituted and empowered the Church.

In Closing

We see so many church staff members falling left and right after going toe to toe with the enemy. Yet if we look at the truth of the matter, our church members are no different. What I've outlined here in this appendix is actually much the same way I would handle anyone struggling in their chains to any sin. In our desire to be "good," we too often look at others without first taking a holy look at ourselves. The issue is not whose sin is worse; the issue is that *no sin* is any better than the next in the light of holiness.

It is for the hurting, the wounded, the angry, the rejected, the addicted, yet through Jesus the redeemed, the free, the forgiven, the loved, the people like me, that I wrote this book. Give grace. Give mercy. Give forgiveness. Give compassion. Give love. Give hope.

Steps for Dealing with Moral Failure of Staff:

1. Understand Their Sin is No Worse than Your Own

2. Tell Truth to Congregation

3. Lead Through the Circumstance, Don't Avoid It

4. Use As an Opportunity to Teach Confession, Forgiveness & Restoration to Church

5. Teach and Establish an Ethos of Confession to Fellow Christians

Appendix B
Additional Bible Verses

These lists are not exhaustive by any means! Neither have I added verses for every single chapter as some could overlap. I have simply included some of my favorites that have touched my heart as I have traveled this journey before you. Memorize these or just hang them on your bathroom mirror in places where you will see them. (No, I don't have them all memorized either!) Let them speak to you and encourage you. I'm so glad you let me share the hope that I've found with you!

All verses are from the New Living Translation (NLT) except where marked.

The Love of God (Ch.1)

For this is how God loved the world: He gave his one and only Son, so that everyone who believes in him will not perish but have eternal life. - John 3:16

My old self has been crucified with Christ. It is no longer I who live, but Christ lives in me. So I live in this earthly body by trusting in the Son of God, who loved me and gave himself for me. - Galatians 2:20

For the lord your God is living among you. He is a mighty savior. He will take delight in you with gladness. With his love, he will calm all your fears. He will rejoice over you with joyful songs. - Zephaniah 3:17

Yes, God sings over you! :-)

So humble yourselves under the mighty power of God, and at the right time he will lift you up in honor. Give all your worries and cares to God, for he cares about you. - 1 Peter 5:6-7

But you, O Lord, are a God of compassion and mercy, slow to get angry and filled with unfailing love and faithfulness. - Psalm 86:15

And may you have the power to understand, as all God's people should, how wide, how long, how high, and how deep his love is. - Ephesians 3:18

For the lord corrects those he loves, just as a father corrects a child in whom he delights. - Proverbs 3:12

And I am convinced that nothing can ever separate us from God's love. Neither death nor life, neither angels nor demons, neither our fears for today nor our worries about tomorrow—not even the powers of hell can separate us from God's love. No power in the sky above or in the earth below—indeed, nothing in all creation will ever be able to separate us from the love of God that is revealed in Christ Jesus our Lord. - Romans 8:38-39

Grace (Ch.2)

Instead of shame and dishonor, you will enjoy a double share of honor. You will possess a double portion of prosperity in your land, and everlasting joy will be yours. - Isaiah 61:7

For God saved us and called us to live a holy life. He did this, not because we deserved it, but because that was his plan from before the beginning of time—to show us his grace through Christ Jesus. - 2 Timothy 1:9

He is so rich in kindness and grace that he purchased our freedom with the blood of his Son and forgave our sins. - Ephesians 1:7

I do not treat the grace of God as meaningless. For if keeping the law could make us right with God, then there was no need for Christ to die. - Galatians 2:21

Well then, should we keep on sinning so that God can show us more and more of his wonderful grace? Of course not! Since we have died to sin, how can we continue to live in it? - Romans 6:1-2

God saved you by his grace when you believed. And you can't take credit for this; it is a gift from God. - Ephesians 2:8

Forgiveness (Ch.6)

Make allowance for each other's faults, and forgive anyone who offends you. Remember, the Lord forgave you, so you must forgive others. - Colossians 3:13

Then he says, "I will never again remember their sins and lawless deeds." And when sins have been forgiven, there is no need to offer any more sacrifices. - Hebrews 10:17-18

And I will forgive their wickedness, and I will never again remember their sins. - Hebrews 8:12

He has removed our sins as far from us as the east is from the west. - Psalm 103:12

I—yes, I alone—will blot out your sins for my own sake and will never think of them again. - Isaiah 43:25

Just think how much more the blood of Christ will purify our consciences from sinful deeds so that we can worship the living God. For by the power of the eternal Spirit, Christ offered himself to God as a perfect sacrifice for our sins. - Hebrews 9:14

He is so rich in kindness and grace that he purchased our freedom with the blood of his Son and forgave our sins. - Ephesians 1:7

The Mind (Ch.7)

I appeal to you, dear brothers and sisters, by the authority of our Lord Jesus Christ, to live in harmony with each other. Let there be no divisions in the church. Rather, be of one mind, united in thought and purpose. - 1 Corinthians 1:10

Don't copy the behavior and customs of this world, but let God transform you into a new person by changing the way you think. Then you will learn to know God's will for you, which is good and pleasing and perfect. - Romans 12:2

And now, dear brothers and sisters, one final thing. Fix your thoughts on what is true, and honorable, and right, and pure, and lovely, and admirable. Think about things that are excellent and worthy of praise. - Philippians 4:8

Don't worry about anything; instead, pray about everything. Tell God what you need, and thank him for all he has done. - Philippians 4:6

Temptation comes from our own desires, which entice us and drag us away. These desires give birth to sinful actions. And when sin is allowed to grow, it gives birth to death. - James 1:14-15

We are human, but we don't wage war as humans do. We use God's mighty weapons, not worldly weapons, to knock down the strongholds of human reasoning and to destroy false arguments. We destroy every proud obstacle that keeps people from knowing God. We capture their rebellious thoughts and teach them to obey Christ. - 2 Corinthians 10:3-5

Hope (Ch.9)

I am counting on the lord; yes, I am counting on him. I have put my hope in his word. - Psalm 130:5

I pray that your hearts will be flooded with light so that you can understand the confident hope he has given to those he called—his holy people who are his rich and glorious inheritance. - Ephesians 1:18

We can rejoice, too, when we run into problems and trials, for we know that they help us develop endurance. And endurance develops strength of character, and character strengthens our confident hope of salvation. And this hope will not lead to disappointment. For we know how dearly God loves us, because he has given us the Holy Spirit to fill our hearts with his love. - Romans 5:3-5

So be strong and courageous, all you who put your hope in the lord! - Psalm 31:24

But those who hope in the Lord will renew their strength. They will soar on wings like eagles; they will run and not grow weary, they will walk and not be faint. - Isaiah 40:31 (NIV)

For I know the plans I have for you," declares the Lord, "plans to prosper you and not to harm you, plans to give you hope and a future. - Jeremiah 29:11 (NIV)

Why am I discouraged? Why is my heart so sad? I will put my hope in God! I will praise him again—my Savior and my God! - Psalm 42:11

And so, Lord, where do I put my hope? My only hope is in you. - Psalm 39:7

For there is one body and one Spirit, just as you have been called to one glorious hope for the future. - Ephesians 4:4

Let us hold tightly without wavering to the hope we affirm, for God can be trusted to keep his promise. - Hebrews 10:23

Notes

Chapter 2

1. Max Lucado, *In the Grip of Grace,* (Nashville: Thomas Nelson, 1996), digital book

Chapter 7

1. Rascal Flatts, Phillip White and D. Vincent Williams, *I'm Moving On.* MP3, 4:06. 2000.

2. Allen Asbury, Darrell R. Brown and Ty Lacy, *Somebody's Praying Me Through,* MP3, 4:04. 2002.